Direct Mail
FOR
DUMMIES®

by Richard Goldsmith

with
Dan Breau, Sandra Blackthorn,
and Kelly Ewing

IDG
BOOKS
WORLDWIDE

IDG Books Worldwide, Inc.
An International Data Group Company

Foster City, CA ✦ Chicago, IL ✦ Indianapolis, IN ✦ New York, NY

Direct Mail For Dummies®

Published by
IDG Books Worldwide, Inc.
An International Data Group Company
919 E. Hillsdale Blvd.
Suite 400
Foster City, CA 94404
www.idgbooks.com (IDG Books Worldwide Web site)
www.dummies.com (Dummies Press Web site)

Library of Congress Control Number: 00-105651

ISBN: 0-7645-0764-8

Printed in the United States of America

10 9 8 7 6 5 4 3 2 1

1O/RS/QX/QQ/IN

Distributed in the United States by IDG Books Worldwide, Inc.

Distributed by CDG Books Canada Inc. for Canada; by Transworld Publishers Limited in the United Kingdom; by IDG Norge Books for Norway; by IDG Sweden Books for Sweden; by IDG Books Australia Publishing Corporation Pty. Ltd. for Australia and New Zealand; by TransQuest Publishers Pte Ltd. for Singapore, Malaysia, Thailand, Indonesia, and Hong Kong; by Gotop Information Inc. for Taiwan; by ICG Muse, Inc. for Japan; by Intersoft for South Africa; by Eyrolles for France; by International Thomson Publishing for Germany, Austria and Switzerland; by Distribuidora Cuspide for Argentina; by LR International for Brazil; by Galileo Libros for Chile; by Ediciones ZETA S.C.R. Ltda. for Peru; by WS Computer Publishing Corporation, Inc., for the Philippines; by Contemporanea de Ediciones for Venezuela; by Express Computer Distributors for the Caribbean and West Indies; by Micronesia Media Distributor, Inc. for Micronesia; by Chips Computadoras S.A. de C.V. for Mexico; by Editorial Norma de Panama S.A. for Panama; by American Bookshops for Finland.

For general information on IDG Books Worldwide's books in the U.S., please call our Consumer Customer Service department at 800-762-2974. For reseller information, including discounts and premium sales, please call our Reseller Customer Service department at 800-434-3422.

For information on where to purchase IDG Books Worldwide's books outside the U.S., please contact our International Sales department at 317-596-5530 or fax 317-572-4002.

For consumer information on foreign language translations, please contact our Customer Service department at 1-800-434-3422, fax 317-572-4002, or e-mail rights@idgbooks.com.

For information on licensing foreign or domestic rights, please phone 650-653-7098.

For sales inquiries and special prices for bulk quantities, please contact our Order Services department at 800-434-3422 or write to the address above.

For information on using IDG Books Worldwide's books in the classroom or for ordering examination copies, please contact our Educational Sales department at 800-434-2086 or fax 317-572-4005.

For press review copies, author interviews, or other publicity information, please contact our Public Relations department at 650-653-7000 or fax 650-653-7500.

For authorization to photocopy items for corporate, personal, or educational use, please contact Copyright Clearance Center, 222 Rosewood Drive, Danvers, MA 01923, or fax 978-750-4470.

About the Authors

Richard Goldsmith: Richard Goldsmith has been in the direct marketing and printing industry for 20 years. In 1981, he founded the Horah Group and is Chairman of Horah Direct, a full service Direct Marketing agency and a partner in PGI Mailers, a Lettershop/Bindery in New Ulm, Minnesota. Dick is a member of the Direct Marketing Association, as well as Women in Direct Marketing International. A well known speaker, he has presented at numerous DMA Annual Conferences, Direct Marketing Days in New York and Minneapolis, and for the Direct Marketing Clubs of Seattle and St. Louis. Dick has had numerous articles published in *Target Marketing* magazine and *Circulation Management* magazine. He can be reached at 212-921-4521 or e-mail `Dick@Horah.com`.

Dan Breau: Dan Breau has been in direct marketing since 1969 as a copywriter, creative director, strategic planner, and agency principal. He has developed successful strategic and creative solutions for such companies as Volvo, Citibank, Mutual of Omaha, Time-Life, Johnson & Johnson, and American Airlines. His awards include an Echo Award from the DMA, a Gold Best of Show from WDMI for *Investor's Business Daily*, and a Gold Medal from the NJ Ad Club for *BusinessWeek*.

Sandra Blackthorn: Sandra Blackthorn has a degree in journalism and has been involved with the editorial side of book publishing since 1987. In 1992, Sandra hooked up with IDG Books Worldwide, Inc., and became the pivotal editor in defining and refining what the *...For Dummies* series has become. Nowadays, she runs her own freelance editorial and writing business. And when she's not grappling (lovingly) with words, she's grappling (even more lovingly) with her husband, David, and spirited children, William and Katie. And, yes, *spirited* is a euphemism.

Kelly Ewing: Kelly Ewing is a writer and editor who lives in Greenwood, Indiana, with her husband Mark, daughter Katie, and two dogs, Cheyenne and Sierra. Kelly edits numerous bestsellers for the award-winning *...For Dummies* series, has coauthored a computer book, and is currently writing a business book. She has also written articles on sports, travel, and human interest for several newspapers.

ABOUT IDG BOOKS WORLDWIDE

Welcome to the world of IDG Books Worldwide.

IDG Books Worldwide, Inc., is a subsidiary of International Data Group, the world's largest publisher of computer-related information and the leading global provider of information services on information technology. IDG was founded more than 30 years ago by Patrick J. McGovern and now employs more than 9,000 people worldwide. IDG publishes more than 290 computer publications in over 75 countries. More than 90 million people read one or more IDG publications each month.

Launched in 1990, IDG Books Worldwide is today the #1 publisher of best-selling computer books in the United States. We are proud to have received eight awards from the Computer Press Association in recognition of editorial excellence and three from Computer Currents' First Annual Readers' Choice Awards. Our best-selling ...For Dummies® series has more than 50 million copies in print with translations in 31 languages. IDG Books Worldwide, through a joint venture with IDG's Hi-Tech Beijing, became the first U.S. publisher to publish a computer book in the People's Republic of China. In record time, IDG Books Worldwide has become the first choice for millions of readers around the world who want to learn how to better manage their businesses.

Our mission is simple: Every one of our books is designed to bring extra value and skill-building instructions to the reader. Our books are written by experts who understand and care about our readers. The knowledge base of our editorial staff comes from years of experience in publishing, education, and journalism — experience we use to produce books to carry us into the new millennium. In short, we care about books, so we attract the best people. We devote special attention to details such as audience, interior design, use of icons, and illustrations. And because we use an efficient process of authoring, editing, and desktop publishing our books electronically, we can spend more time ensuring superior content and less time on the technicalities of making books.

You can count on our commitment to deliver high-quality books at competitive prices on topics you want to read about. At IDG Books Worldwide, we continue in the IDG tradition of delivering quality for more than 30 years. You'll find no better book on a subject than one from IDG Books Worldwide.

John Kilcullen
Chairman and CEO
IDG Books Worldwide, Inc.

VIII
WINNER

*Eighth Annual
Computer Press
Awards ≥1992*

IX
WINNER

*Ninth Annual
Computer Press
Awards ≥1993*

X
WINNER

*Tenth Annual
Computer Press
Awards ≥1994*

XI
WINNER

*Eleventh Annual
Computer Press
Awards ≥1995*

IDG is the world's leading IT media, research and exposition company. Founded in 1964, IDG had 1997 revenues of $2.05 billion and has more than 9,000 employees worldwide. IDG offers the widest range of media options that reach IT buyers in 75 countries representing 95% of worldwide IT spending. IDG's diverse product and services portfolio spans six key areas including print publishing, online publishing, expositions and conferences, market research, education and training, and global marketing services. More than 90 million people read one or more of IDG's 290 magazines and newspapers, including IDG's leading global brands — Computerworld, PC World, Network World, Macworld and the Channel World family of publications. IDG Books Worldwide is one of the fastest-growing computer book publishers in the world, with more than 700 titles in 36 languages. The "...For Dummies®" series alone has more than 50 million copies in print. IDG offers online users the largest network of technology-specific Web sites around the world through IDG.net (http://www.idg.net), which comprises more than 225 targeted Web sites in 55 countries worldwide. International Data Corporation (IDC) is the world's largest provider of information technology data, analysis and consulting, with research centers in over 41 countries and more than 400 research analysts worldwide. IDG World Expo is a leading producer of more than 168 globally branded conferences and expositions in 35 countries including E3 (Electronic Entertainment Expo), Macworld Expo, ComNet, Windows World Expo, ICE (Internet Commerce Expo), Agenda, DEMO, and Spotlight. IDG's training subsidiary, ExecuTrain, is the world's largest computer training company, with more than 230 locations worldwide and 785 training courses. IDG Marketing Services helps industry-leading IT companies build international brand recognition by developing global integrated marketing programs via IDG's print, online and exposition products worldwide. Further information about the company can be found at www.idg.com.   1/26/00

Publisher's Acknowledgments

We're proud of this book; please register your comments through our IDG Books Worldwide Online Registration Form located at http://my2cents.dummies.com.

Some of the people who helped bring this book to market include the following:

Acquisitions, Editorial, and Media Development

Project Editor: Tracy Barr

Editorial Assistant: Sarah Shupert, Candace Nicholson

Product Marketing Manager: Melisa Duffy

Production

Project Coordinator: Melissa Ward

Layout and Graphics: Brian Drumm, Barry Offringa, Tracy K. Oliver, Dan Whetstine, Erin Zeltner

Proofreader: Brian Massey

Indexer: Sharon Hilgenberg

General and Administrative

IDG Books Worldwide, Inc.: John Kilcullen, CEO

IDG Books Technology Publishing Group: Richard Swadley, Senior Vice President and Publisher; Walter R. Bruce III, Vice President and Publisher; Joseph Wikert, Vice President and Publisher; Mary Bednarek, Vice President and Director, Product Development; Andy Cummings, Publishing Director, General User Group; Mary C. Corder, Editorial Director; Barry Pruett, Publishing Director

IDG Books Consumer Publishing Group: Roland Elgey, Senior Vice President and Publisher; Kathleen A. Welton, Vice President and Publisher; Kevin Thornton, Acquisitions Manager; Kristin A. Cocks, Editorial Director

IDG Books Internet Publishing Group: Brenda McLaughlin, Senior Vice President and Publisher; Sofia Marchant, Online Marketing Manager

IDG Books Production for Branded Press: Debbie Stailey, Director of Production; Cindy L. Phipps, Manager of Project Coordination, Production Proofreading, and Indexing; Tony Augsburger, Manager of Prepress, Reprints, and Systems; Laura Carpenter, Production Control Manager; Shelley Lea, Supervisor of Graphics and Design; Debbie J. Gates, Production Systems Specialist; Robert Springer, Supervisor of Proofreading; Kathie Schutte, Production Supervisor

Packaging and Book Design: Patty Page, Manager, Promotions Marketing

◆

The publisher would like to give special thanks to Patrick J. McGovern, without whom this book would not have been possible.

◆

Table of Contents

ELetter Makes Direct Mail Easy

ELetter is the first Internet-based full-service mailing solution that lets businesses send real mail, 24 hours a day, from their desktops. ELetter allows you to produce the professional high-quality mailings this book covers.

You've decided direct marketing is a strategy you want to use. ELetter makes the job easy.

Before going to the Web and having your mail magically produced, you have to do some up-front work. You have to decide what your offer is and how you're going to communicate it (letters, postcards, flyers, or booklets). Remember, the offer must be compelling, and it must have immediacy. You also have to know whom you want to send the offer to. Remember, direct mail is a three-legged stool: list, offer, copy.

So you sit down and write your communication. Show it to friends and business associates and make sure it says what you want. Make sure it tells the reader why your product or service will be of use to them — the benefits. Make sure you've turned your features into benefits.

Add into the document your letterhead and any graphics you want to use. If you're using pictures, make sure they are scanned at between 300–600 dpi. Save the entire document on your computer.

If the offer is being sent to some or all of your current customers, you already have the "list." Make sure it is in Comma Separated Value, Access, Excel, or dbf format. If you are going to use a compiled list, you can rent those names once you've logged onto ELetter. If you are going to use a response list, you must contact a list broker or go to one of the Web sites that have those lists available and order them. Remember, the list must be in one of the four formats previously mentioned.

It's now time to log onto www.eletter.com. You'll discover many tools to price your mailing, download design layout templates, purchase a mailing list, order a free proof, or check the status of a previous order.

Select what you will be mailing — a letter, postcard, flyer, or booklet. Once again, you'll be offered the option of learning more about the format you've selected, ordering a free proof, or going ahead with your mailing.

From there, you'll need to upload your list (whether it's your own or one you've purchased). Simply click the Browse button and find the list — the one you want to mail to. For that personal look, ELetter will automatically prepare mail merge letters. (Make sure that your document has been prepared using the mail merge feature of Microsoft Word.)

ELetter will automatically clean and standardize your names after they are uploaded. You will be shown a summary of all the corrections that were made, and you can view them individually if you like. You also have the option of using the original name and address, as you entered it, if for some reason you want to do so.

Now, it's time to upload your actual document. ELetter will show you what your document will look like so that you can be sure that the layout is what you want. You can order a FREE printed proof to be mailed to you. Then, once you approve your mailing, you automatically go to the pricing section.

You now select the kind of paper you want to use. With letters, flyers, and booklets, you have five different options. Post cards have two options: high quality glossy cards or white vellum finish cards.

The pricing section of the ELetter Web site knows how many names you've uploaded. After you decide on first class or standard mail, it tells you exactly what your mailing will cost with the desired paper option. You can switch papers and see how that affects your price.

If you want to get the price of the mailing before you start any uploads, you can do so. Simply go to the pricing section immediately. Select the paper you want to use, the number of pages you'll be printing, and how much ink you'll be using. The pricing calculator will tell you the exact cost of printing and mailing, plus postage.

ELetter uses the latest digital printing and mailing technology to do everything else. No effort or time is required on your part to supervise the printing, folding, stuffing, or mailing. Their systems ensure that every piece will be mailed.

ELetter's electronic systems allow you to mail first class letters at reduced rates. By automatically commingling your mail, you get the advantages that BIG mailers get, greatly reducing your costs.

You can save even more money by mailing at bulk rates. As long as your mailing contains 200 pieces, ELetter will qualify and sort your mail according to postal regulations.

Your time is precious, so ELetter's Web-based service is available anytime, anywhere. All you need is access to the Internet and a Web browser. You can devote your time to your business because using ELetter only takes a few minutes. You don't have to spend time printing, folding, addressing, and mailing. Best of all, everything looks very professional.

ELetter does, indeed, make direct mail easy!

Introduction

● ●

*W*hether you're new to direct mail or experienced with it, *Direct Mail For Dummies* is for you. This easy-to-understand book guides you through the direct mail process, pointing out tips and faux pas along the way.

If you're new to direct mail, you'll find information about this powerful, cost-effective sales tool. And if you've tried your hand at direct mail and weren't as successful as you would have liked, this book can help you make a success of your next direct mail campaign.

About This Book

Direct Mail For Dummies is an action-oriented book for action-oriented people. Forget theory — we tell you what works and how you can duplicate it. You discover essential response boosters and testing strategies and find out how you can conquer new target markets affordably. In short, you get a formula for a successful direct mail campaign.

Direct Mail For Dummies shows you how to plan, create, manage, and control your own direct mail campaigns. In no time, you'll be saving time and money thanks to your successful direct mail campaigns.

Foolish Assumptions

In writing this book, we made some assumptions about you:

- ✔ You already know something about advertising, marketing, selling, and even using direct mail.

- ✔ You may have tried a direct mail campaign that wasn't as efficient, cost-effective, and profitable as you would have liked it to be.

- ✔ You're eager to discover the ins and outs of direct mail. Fortunately, that's what we give you in this book.

How This Book Is Organized

Just like every great direct mail campaign, every great book needs a plan. We divided this book into four parts, each with chapters pertaining to that part so that you can easily find the information that you need.

Part I: Direct Mail Does Work!

If you're new to direct mail, then you'll probably want to read this part. We tell you how direct mail can help your business and how to determine whether direct mail is even right for you. Then we give you a 12-step program to help you successfully launch your direct mail campaign.

Part II: Developing Your Game Plan

For a direct mail campaign to succeed, you need to know what you want to happen. You can't just haphazardly make decisions as you go along. In this part, you find out how to determine your offer, your target audience, and your direct mail piece format. We also give you tips on writing, designing, and printing your direct mail piece.

Part III: Ready, Send, Results!

If all systems are go, then you're ready to drop your direct mail piece in the mail. But not so fast. You need to standardize your addresses, merge and purge your mailing list, and decide how you want to send your piece. Then, once your direct mail piece is in the hands of your customers, you need to measure your results. Of course, we tell you how to do that, too.

Part IV: The Part of Tens

The short, lighthearted chapters in this part tell you who should be using direct mail and why you don't have to worry about the Internet ever thwarting your direct mail efforts.

Icons Used in This Book

Throughout the book, you'll notice little symbols in the margin. These symbols, known as *icons,* mark important points that you'll want to note.

This bull's eye appears next to shortcuts and tips that make your work easier.

When you see this icon, be sure that you read the paragraph. This icon warns you of common mistakes and ways to avoid them.

This icon marks any point you'll want to be sure to remember. You may want to reread these paragraphs.

Where to Go from Here

As interesting as this book is, you won't hurt our feelings if you don't read it from cover to cover. In fact, we wrote this book with the thought that you probably wouldn't read everything in it. That's okay. *Direct Mail For Dummies* is a reference book, after all. Simply use the Index or the Table of Contents to look up the topic you want more information on and then turn to the relevant pages.

Where you start in this book depends largely on where you are in your direct mail campaign. If you've never done a campaign before, for example, you may want to start with Part I. If you have your direct mail piece finished and are ready to print, Chapter 8 would be a good place for you. Or, if you've completed your first mail campaign and what to know how you fared, then check out Chapter 10.

Part I
Direct Mail Does Work!

In this part . . .

You have this book in your hands, so you're probably convinced that direct mail is a good thing. But you probably don't realize all of the many ways direct mail can help your business. And despite its vast benefits, direct mail doesn't always end up being for everyone.

In this part, we tell you all this and more. We even give you a 12-step program for your most successful direct mail campaign ever.

Chapter 1

How Direct Mail Helps Businesses (Getting the Facts Straight)

*Y*ou've known about direct mail since you were a kid. And you've definitely gotten your share of it in the mailbox through the years. Now you're a business person, and you're seriously considering using direct mail to make your business grow.

What you want to do first, though, is get some facts straight. You want to make sure you know the differences between direct marketing, direct mail, and advertising. You want to know if direct mail really is effective. You want some statistics about direct mail. And you want to know which kinds of products work through direct mail and which don't. You've come to the right place. This chapter sorts it all out.

Aren't Direct Marketing and Direct Mail the Same Thing?

No, they're not exactly the same thing. Here's the scoop in a nutshell: Direct marketing is a method of selling, and direct mail is just one medium used in direct marketing. Lots of other popular direct marketing media are also used — things like

- ✔ Mail order, which are ads with *response devices* in them — things like coupons, phone numbers, fax numbers, e-mail addresses, and Internet addresses

- ✔ Radio and TV commercials that ask for an order and include response devices (usually a toll-free number)

- ✔ Catalogs, which offer you products to buy directly from the merchant

- ✔ Insert cards in magazines, which are extremely effective and inexpensive to produce and distribute

- ✔ Card decks, which present you with many different offers from many marketers all in one package of cards

- ✔ Package inserts, which are little flyers or brochures placed in billing statements or in the boxes of products that are delivered by mail

- ✔ Free-standing inserts (FSIs), usually inserted in newspapers, with response devices in them

- ✔ Internet banner ads placed on Web sites that invite you to "Click Here" to place an order

- ✔ Opt-in e-mail, which is sent by marketers to e-mail addresses with an offer and which incurs no printing and postage costs

Less frequently used direct marketing media include counter displays with Take One cards to mail in and even matchbook covers that make an offer and provide a tiny coupon and a toll-free number.

But of all these media, direct mail is the leader in terms of the number of people reached annually and in terms of consistent success. The reason? Direct mail is an extremely targetable, powerful, and cost-effective medium — and it's won wide consumer acceptance.

Entire businesses have been built almost entirely on direct mail. Think of the huge book and record clubs, like the Book-of-the-Month Club, the Literary Guild, Columbia House, RCA Record Club, BMG Music Service, and Time-Life Books. These companies rely heavily on direct mail to acquire customers and also depend on the mail to deliver their merchandise — a complete mail-based channel of distribution.

Thousands of companies use direct mail to sell and service customers. Globe Insurance sells millions of dollars of insurance without any sales agents. Many merchants rely on a specialty form of direct mail called catalogs to sell their wares — things like knick knacks from Lillian Vernon, apparel from Land's End and L.L. Bean, premium fruit from Harry and David, roses from Jackson & Perkins, gourmet coffees from Gevalia, and even prime cuts of beef from Omaha Steaks.

Why Is Direct Mail So Effective?

Direct mail works because it's a *personal* medium.

Okay, granted, there are more personal methods. The most personal, but also most costly, selling medium is face-to-face communication — talking one on one to someone. Retailers in small stores have this advantage. They can greet and talk to their customers, smile, and offer help. Sales people in business-to-business environments and professionals who provide services also rely heavily on personal communication.

The next most personal medium is the phone call. But think about when you've gotten some of those sales calls — during dinner, when you've got the kids in the tub, when you're heading out the door for an appointment. Sometimes a sales call is an intrusion, and it has to be handled very carefully to be successful.

So consider this:

> ✔ A letter in the mail is personal, too. People love getting mail that addresses their interests and needs. It's a way for them to connect to other people and a way for them to get news that's personal or that provides them with helpful ideas and information.

✔ Mail is *tactile*. Your customer can touch it, handle it, unfold it, get involved in it. No other medium offers this level of personal, physical contact with your sales message.

✔ And even though today's consumers are media savvy and besieged with advertising and sales appeals, they still have a feeling of control when they get the day's mail. They can catch their breath for a moment, sort through the mail, and select what they want to open and read first. They have a sense of anticipation — a "what's in it for me" curiosity.

When your direct mail promises to satisfy that curiosity, you're suddenly a welcome visitor in a person's home or office. And you're talking to him or her *personally*.

Always keep your message personal. Chapter 7 covers how to design your direct mail piece and how to make sure that your message is personal, friendly, and conversational.

How Big Is Direct Mail?

We're talking *huge*. According to a 1999 Direct Marketing Association (DMA) study, direct mail in the United States alone is a $40 billion industry. And for the past 20 years, it's been growing at a compounded growth rate of more than 6 percent — an indication of the steadily increasing acceptance of targeted direct mail among consumers and businesses. No other marketing communications medium has grown so fast for so long a time.

You can sell *anything* through the mail. But what separates the winners from the losers is the ability to sell *profitably.* That's where this book comes in. It gives tested and proven techniques and shortcuts that will launch you quickly to the top of the learning curve with direct mail.

The Things That Don't Succeed

You need to know up front that there are some things you generally can't sell profitably through direct mail — *commodity items,* products that are readily available in stores.

Okay, we hear ya: "But there are lots of book and record stores around. How come the book and record clubs succeed?" Well, because they carved out a niche selling at a discount and offering an entry-level transaction that retail outlets can't profitably match: three books for a buck or ten CDs for a penny. They capture customers this way and can predict to a fare-thee-well what the lifetime value of a customer is.

For example, book and record clubs calculate how much they can afford to give away up front to acquire a customer, how long on average it takes to recoup that cost and break even, and how long a customer will remain a member and keep buying before quitting. In short, they calculate — by keeping very careful records — the lifetime value of a customer.

Note that online book retailers, such as Amazon.com, are not running a "club" business. Like retail stores, they wait for customers to come to them. The book and record clubs are proactive. They aggressively promote memberships and send regular announcements to members to buy.

Besides the book and record clubs, there are other successful direct mail sellers of commodity items. Take fruit, for example. You can buy fresh fruit in any grocery or supermarket. So how do Harry and David sell fruit profitably by mail? They deal in specialty gourmet fruit, the kind you can't readily find in stores. What's more, they present their fruit in such mouth-watering terms that it's irresistible to certain people — an upscale target market of people who are willing to pay a hefty premium for exclusivity and top quality.

And so it goes for other successful direct mail sellers of commodity products. They have found a distinction in their product category, or they have created a distinction that appeals to certain segments of the population. (Check out Chapter 5 for suggestions on identifying your target audience.)

The Difference between Direct Marketing and Advertising

Many, many people think that advertising and direct marketing/ direct mail are the exact same thing. It's such a common misconception that we want to take a minute to set the record straight.

Advertising — so-called general advertising — is *not* a method of selling or a channel of distribution. Advertising is a form of marketing communications. General advertising and direct marketing can work well together at times, especially when campaigns in each medium are integrated in terms of targeting and timing.

The objectives of general advertising differ from those of direct marketing — and from direct mail. Advertising seeks to create, build, or maintain an awareness of and a desire for a product or service. Advertising, done well, can *support* the selling process. But its goal has only three main parts: gain *Attention*, stimulate *Interest*, and provoke *Desire (AID)*. Advertising is an *aid* in the selling process. You certainly want people to pay attention, take an interest in what you have to sell, and desire it enough to buy. But to take the next step, your prospect has to go the store. (A store, a retailer, is a *channel of distribution*. If you're a package goods manufacturer or reseller of detergent, soup, pantyhose, toothpaste, picture hooks, whatever, or if you make things like apparel, automobiles, and refrigerators, you need to get your merchandise into a store of some kind so that consumers can buy it. Otherwise, all the attention, interest, and desire you've spent zillions on will be wasted.)

On the flip side, direct marketing is not only a form of marketing communications, but it is also a channel of distribution. That's why it's ideal for small entrepreneurial businesses as well as big established companies. With direct marketing, you don't need a store or showroom. You may need a warehouse, but in some cases you don't even need that. (If you can get a manufacturer to drop-ship merchandise to your customers, all you do is make the sale through one or more direct marketing media, take the orders, tell the manufacturer who to ship to, and deposit the checks.) So the difference between advertising and direct marketing is *Action*.

The goal of direct marketing/direct mail has four parts: Attention, Interest, Desire, and Action — or AIDA. (Ever heard of Giuseppi Verdi's famous opera called *Aida?* Aida is the name of the heroine. She not only gained the *attention* of her boyfriend, Radames, but she also stimulated his *interest*, provoked his *desire*, and got him to take *action.)*

Action is the fourth and critical point of difference between general advertising and direct marketing/direct mail. An ad stops after the first three steps — attention, interest, and desire. Direct marketing and direct mail urge the prospect or customer to take action, and they provide the means to do so.

Direct marketing and direct mail provide an order form or a coupon, a phone or fax number, or a Web site or an e-mail address so the consumer can actually respond to the offer right then and there — without going to the store. In effect, you take the store — or the opportunity — to the customer.

Chapter 2

How Do I Know If Direct Mail Is Right for Me?

*T*oo often, folks jump blindly onto the Anything That'll Grow My Business bandwagon without first considering whether the choice is really right for their needs or products. Don't be one of those folks. Read this chapter so you can figure out whether direct mail is the right approach for you and your business.

Nailing Down Your Goals

Before you can pursue any project successfully, you need to have a plan — to know exactly what you want to do and to make sure that you stay focused on your objective.

Objectives are specific, measurable goals for a period of time. They should also be attainable. (The great football coach Vince Lombardi used to tell his players that he wanted them to take the ball and use four tries to go ten yards. He said that if they just keep doing that, the touchdowns will come.)

Strategies are the planned actions you take to reach your objectives. Direct marketing is a strategy. "I will use direct marketing to sell 5,000 sewing machines."

A no-win direct mail scenario

If you have only one product that lasts a long time — an unabridged dictionary, for example — and it sells for $24.95, you will probably never make money in direct mail. It's too expensive. The lifetime value of your customer is $24.95 less the cost of goods sold. The cost of acquiring that customer through direct mail will probably be much higher.

Tactics are the details of how you will execute the strategies. "I will use a direct mail package with a letter, a colorful brochure, and an order card to sell those sewing machines. As a premium to order within the next seven days, I will offer a free book on how to use the sewing machine to create beautiful clothes and domestic items at half of what you'd pay for them in a store. I will send these direct mail packages to people who subscribe to sewing magazines."

In order to know whether your objectives are realistic — and whether direct marketing and direct mail are the right strategy and tactic to use — you have to know your market:

- ✔ Who are your potential customers?
- ✔ How many are there?
- ✔ How do they typically buy your product or service?
- ✔ How much of your product or service can they use?
- ✔ What is the lifetime value of a new customer?
- ✔ Who's your competition? What are they doing?

How do you find out the answers to these questions? Research. Sorry — there's no easy way around it.

Conducting research can be time consuming and expensive, but you gotta do it. Otherwise, you may end up spending a lot of money on a direct mail campaign that'll never be profitable.

Doing Your Research

The good news is that you can conduct some very meaningful research without much expense. This section covers a few do-it-yourself ideas. After you do your research, you can decide whether direct mail is the tactic that will help you accomplish your goals.

Talk to customers on the phone

If you currently sell a certain product, call some of your customers and ask them these questions:

- ✔ What do you like best about the product? What do you like least?
- ✔ Would you buy it again?
- ✔ Where did you buy the product?
- ✔ Would you recommend it to friends or associates?
- ✔ How has it helped you?
- ✔ Do you have ideas on how it can be improved?

You also need to get some personal info about your customers. What kind of info to get differs a bit depending on whether you're selling to businesses or to consumers.

If you're selling to consumers, try to get personal info like this:

- ✔ Whether they're male or female
- ✔ Where they live
- ✔ Whether they're employed or retired
- ✔ What their income is
- ✔ How educated they are
- ✔ How old they are
- ✔ Whether they have kids and, if so, how many
- ✔ How they spend their leisure time

- ✔ Whether they're members of a group – ethnic, religious, professional, etc.
- ✔ Whether they support a political party
- ✔ Whether they donate money to charity
- ✔ What they've purchased through the mail

And if you're selling to business customers, try to get personal info like this:

- ✔ Where they work
- ✔ What kind of company they work for (the SIC, or Standard Industrial Classification, code)
- ✔ What the annual sales of the company are
- ✔ Whether the company is a single-location company
- ✔ Whether they're at a headquarters or division
- ✔ How many employees are in the company
- ✔ What their job or functional title is
- ✔ How old they are
- ✔ How educated they are

Yes, this is all pretty basic stuff, but so many people don't bother asking questions like these. A big mistake.

Send out a survey

After you talk with a number of customers on the phone, you can construct a written survey to mail to people so that you can get even greater input — from a large base of people.

The bottom line is that you have to know who your potential customers are and what channels they use to obtain your product or service. Are they personal consumers or businesses? How do others generate business for the same product or service?

After you get the answers to these questions, write down some realistic goals and think about the strategies you'll use to achieve those goals. If your initial research shows that direct marketing should be one of your strategies for achieving your goals, it's time for more research.

Start filing the direct mail you receive

Keep and file all the direct mail you get in your category. Pay attention to which mailings come again. Read them and study them. See how they describe your products or services and similar ones.

The direct mail you keep and file is your *swipe file,* a valuable resource you can use for ideas and to check the completeness of your own direct mail. Every good practitioner of direct marketing keeps a swipe file.

Do not plagiarize. You can't copy other people's ideas word for word without the risk of being sued. You can, however, study their direct mail carefully and imitate the concepts and structure of what they do.

Consider the costs involved

You need to find out approximately what your direct mail campaign is going to cost. Knowing the costs enables you to determine whether direct mail will allow you to meet your goals.

Besides the research cost, there's the creative cost — writing and designing your direct mail package. You can do it yourself, with the help of this book (see Chapter 7), or you can hire professional help. Professional help can cost anywhere from $1,000 to $50,000. How large is your budget?

You also need to find out what it's going to cost to acquire names, print your materials, and mail your materials. (Chapter 5 talks about getting names, Chapter 8 gets into printing, and Chapter 9 tells you how to get your direct mail piece delivered.)

Chapter 3

Twelve Steps to Direct Mail Success

In This Chapter

▶ Slugging through the 12-step process for creating a direct mail campaign

▶ Understanding what you want to accomplish throughout the process

Some people think that doing direct mail has to be a breeze. You just write up a sales message; print it on a post card, stuff it into an envelope, or put it in a box or tube; and mail it. Then you sit back and wait for the inquiries, orders, and checks to roll in. Right?

Not quite. It's actually more complicated than that. You need to go through a specific process to create direct mail, and that's what this chapter's all about. It gives you an overview of the 12-step program for direct mail success. (Parts II and III of this book cover specific details.)

The Process for Creating Direct Mail

This section outlines the steps to take when planning your direct mail campaign. Since we don't know what your specific product, service, or unique appeal is, use these steps as a general guide or checklist for your own campaign. You undoubtedly will see practical ways to modify these steps to suit your personal needs, so think of them as just a basic recipe to start with.

Here are the key steps of the direct mail process:

1. Choose which product or service to offer.

Write down a complete description. In one column, list the facts about it, ranking them in order from most important to least. In a second column, translate each fact or feature into an end-user benefit.

The features are what the product or service *is*. The benefits are what you *sell*.

(Chapter 4 provides details on determining your offer.)

2. Determine your marketing or sales strategy.

Go through your market research (see Chapter 2) and make sure that you've clearly defined your measurable goals (objectives), planned actions (strategies to meet your goals), and tactics (details for executing your strategies).

3. Identify your target audience.

Write down every characteristic of your audience that matters: gender, age, ethnicity, education, income, occupation, interests, hobbies, children in the household, car(s) owned, pets, vacation and leisure activities, health or disability, and so on. (Refer to Chapter 5 for detailed info on identifying your target audience.)

4. Decide how you want the prospect, customer, or donor to respond.

Memorize this right now: *Make it easy for people to respond.* Regardless of what kind of response device you use (coupons, phone numbers, fax numbers, e-mail addresses, Internet addresses, and so on), you need to make sure that responding is easy.

This is especially important when you devise the offer, write the copy, and design the graphics. Keep asking yourself these questions: Does this headline make it easy for people to respond? Does this word, sentence, or paragraph move the selling process forward to the conclusion I want? Does the overall layout draw the reader in? Do the details of the design guide the reader's eyes easily through the sales message — and right to the ordering device?)

A good test in this industry is to ask a sixth grader to read your direct mail — especially the order form. If a sixth grader can read and understand your direct mail message and actually order what you're selling, you're definitely doing it right.

5. Create the offer.

Write down the offer as you would on an order card included in your direct mail piece (see Chapter 4 for details on determining your offer).

6. Write the rough-draft copy and design the graphics.

Decide on and rough out all the components of your direct mail package. Thumbnail sketches will do at this point, but be sure to include sizes and whether each piece will be one, two, or four colors. (Chapter 7 covers how to design your direct mail piece.)

7. Select the paper and production methods and vendors.

Identify the suppliers you want to work with — for lists, list enhancements, printers, lettershops, free-lancers, or agencies.

Talk to your printer(s) and lettershop and explain what you're planning. Ask how long it will take to print and produce — ready to mail — each component. Often, the envelope takes the longest to produce, especially if you choose one that requires a special die-cut. And any component that requires die-cutting, gluing, peel-off stickers, or special finishing will take extra time.

Your objective is to determine which components take the longest to produce so you can create a reverse timetable and have all the pieces finished and at the lettershop or postal service for mailing on time. Rely on your lettershop or the Postal Service for answers to questions about postal regulations and mailing permits.

Prepare a more detailed graphic layout of each component so you can get price bids from your vendors. It's a good idea to get multiple bids for each piece — and not just one price. You should be concerned with three key elements: price, quality, and ability to deliver on time. Your choice of vendors will probably be based on the appropriate combination of these three factors. Be prepared to wait several days for the bids to come in.

(Chapter 8 covers printing, paper, and ink kinds of things, and Chapter 9 talks about list processing, lettershops, the postal service, and costs.)

8. **Finalize the copy and the graphic design.**

You can hire outside help, like freelancers, a production studio, or a direct mail agency, or you can finalize the copy and design yourself (turn to Chapter 7 for help).

9. **Determine whether you need to test.**

Chapter 10 gets into the details of how to test your direct mail, but here's some quick advice: You can't test if you have a small target market, and it's not worth testing if your market isn't big enough to allow test cells of at least 5,000 names. If you do a three-way test, you'll use up 15,000 names. One test cell will likely come up a winner, but if the total audience is only 25,000 or 30,000 names, you don't have much of a chance to do a confirmation test and a rollout. In cases like this, you need to rely on research and intuition.

10. **Get it mailed.**

Going the postal service route? You need to check into the various postal service specifications and rates. And to ensure proper and rapid processing and delivery of your mail, you need to make sure that your list of people and addresses is up to date.

If you're planning a massive mailing — tens of thousands of pieces, for example — you probably want to use a commercial lettershop to help you get your large mailing into the mail. Chapter 9 is the place to go for details about all these things.

11. **Tally the orders.**

Keep close track of who your orders are coming from. Start a database with the information. Keep track of what people are buying and how much they are spending. All of this information can help you mail smarter next time. Your goal is not only to make a sale but also to make a customer!

12. Fulfill the orders.

Throughout the entire planning process, take the time to think through what you're doing — again and again. Don't rush. Ask yourself, "What's more important — that we do it right now or that we do it right?" Having to do things over wastes time and money.

What You Want the Process to Accomplish

The goal in doing the 12-step program is to trigger a direct action, a measurable action, at the right cost.

The practitioners of general advertising want to create awareness, brand recognition, and desire. These things are *feelings*, not actions, which is a key difference between general advertising and direct mail (see Chapter 2). General advertising rarely uses direct mail because it's too expensive a medium to build awareness.

In direct mail, you obviously want people to feel good about what you're offering. But above all, you want them to *act now*. So memorize this critical question:

What do you want a person in your target audience to do when he or she reads your selling message in the mail?

This question — and your answer — should be the driving force of everything you do in direct mail. You must have a clear answer in your own mind. Then, as you go through the process, you can use this question as a yardstick, a way to check whether all the steps in the process are on track.

Brainstorms can lead to gold mines

Years ago at the Prell shampoo company, someone caught lightning in a bottle. The original instructions on Prell's shampoo bottle said to wash and rinse — just like every other shampoo. But when the directions were changed to "Wash, rinse, repeat," sales of Prell *doubled*.

Always be on the lookout for new ideas. Frequently ask yourself and others, "Is there anything else we can do to the product or the offer to improve it?"

Part II

Developing Your Game Plan

The 5th Wave   By Rich Tennant

WELCOME TO
The Panama Canyon
The First Man Made Canyon
Next to Two Oceans

OOPS!

"Well, this sure changes what we can offer our target customers."

In this part . . .

*1*f you know you want to do direct mail but you're just getting started, then this part is for you. Here, you can find out how to determine what you're going to offer, who your target audience is, and what format your direct mail piece will take. We even give you writing, designing, and printing tips.

Chapter 4

Determining Your Offer

· ·

· ·

*B*ack in days gone by, dairy farmers used a three-legged milking stool. It was strong, sturdy, utilitarian, and perfectly suited for a dairy farmer's task — getting up close and personal to milk the cow. And what happened if one leg of the stool broke? Well . . . kaplooey.

A direct marketing analogy can be made of that same dairy stool: If you want to successfully milk sales, sales leads, profits, donations, or whatever else from your marketplace, you need to make certain that your direct mail campaign sits firmly on the three legs of direct marketing:

  ✔ The strategy (your offer)

  ✔ Targeted mailing lists (your target audience)

  ✔ Tactical and creative execution (your copy and design)

This chapter covers one vital leg — your all-important offer. Chapter 5 covers the second vital leg, and Chapter 7 covers the third.

Understanding What the Offer Is

The offer is the part of your direct mail that attracts attention and builds interest. It's the total selling proposition, the deal, you make to a prospect or customer — the combination of the product or service, the price, and the way you present the two (see the section "Looking at the Components of the Offer," later in this chapter, for more information).

Study your competitors' offers. If you see the same direct mail solicitation being sent two months, six months, or a year down the road, it's a moneymaker. Learn from it.

Choosing the Right Kind of Offer

The choices you make for your offer make a difference in your success — often a huge difference. Here's a little story to help you see how:

Suppose that a manufacturer of thermal-pane replacement windows decides to use direct mail to generate sales leads in his market area — say, Minnesota, where winters are cold and people have a real incentive to save on heating fuel.

Fred, the manufacturer, sends direct mail to homeowners and offers a free indoor-outdoor thermometer to people who let a salesperson come to their home for a demonstration.

The sales leads come in. Lots of them. The salespeople make appointments and try to close deals, but they don't close enough to satisfy Fred. He's been giving away of lot of thermometers, but his salespeople are grumbling that they're wasting time on poor-quality leads.

So Fred decides to mail again. This time, he tests premiums: the same thermometer versus a do-it-yourself home repair book versus a battery-operated fire alarm/smoke detector. Each prospect doesn't receive a mailing that gives a choice of premiums. Instead, Fred divides his second mailing effort into three test cells, each identical except for the premium offered.

The results? In terms of sales leads received, about 45 percent are for the thermometer, 35 percent are for the book, and 20 percent are for the fire alarm/smoke detector.

Again, the sales force goes out. They are phenomenally successful closing deals to the people who responded to the fire alarm/smoke detector offer. Sales to the other two groups are pretty much the same as before — okay but not great.

Fred wonders, "Why the difference?"

To find out, Fred hires a research firm to phone both the people who bought and the people who didn't. Here's what he discovers: The people who responded to the offer for the fire alarm/smoke detector intended to live in their homes for a long time and were therefore interested in protecting the investment in their homes. To them, the free fire alarm/smoke detector symbolized protection. That desire made those people better prospects.

The choices used in the offer made a huge difference. The fire alarm/smoke detector respondents bought windows twice as often as those in the other two groups. Fred discovered that it was more profitable to generate fewer sales leads to people who had a serious intention to buy.

Be persistent. Zone in on the most relevant target market (see Chapter 5) and choose an appropriate offer and incentive to send to that group of potential customers.

Looking at the Basic Components of the Offer

Your offer needs to include specific info that pertains directly to the product (or service) and the price — things like the terms of payment, the time limit for ordering, any incentives, and the guarantee. Various ways are available to present the components of your offer. Here are a few basic tips and possibilities:

- ✔ **Product or service.** Ideally, it should be something generally unavailable in stores. For example, coffee is available in grocery stores, but specialty gourmet coffee is not. The deal a company like Gevalia offers is that its coffees are unique.

- ✔ **Price.** It can be straightforward. Or it can be free. Many business-to-business offers are for free information as Step 1 in the selling process. Step 2 is a follow-up mailing that provides information and makes a product or service offer.

For merchandise, you can offer a free trial, a no-risk trial with a money-back guarantee, a discount, a special sale, a two-for-one deal, a regular version at one price and a deluxe version of the same thing (gold-stamped with the customer's name, for example) at a higher price, or a premium with the order.

✓ **Terms of payment.** You may lose sales if you always ask for full payment. Other options are delayed payments, extended payments, and installment payments. And you can offer a choice of "Bill me," C.O.D. (cash on delivery), credit card, personal check, or money order.

✓ **Time limit.** You can create a sense of urgency by stipulating that orders must be received by a certain date or "within XX days." If your offer is good, people won't want to be left out.

Be careful with the time limit you choose. It shouldn't be too short, or people won't be able to order and meet the date. And it shouldn't be too long, or inertia will set in. Study what your competitors do and imitate them. If you use a time limit, be sure to announce it prominently in the copy — and especially on the order form.

✓ **Incentives.** Incentives are enticements, motivators — things like free premiums or a second item at half price (see the section "Choosing the Right Kind of Offer" for an example).

✓ **Guarantee.** This is the part of the deal that gives your customer confidence to buy and confidence to trust that you stand behind your product. Make the guarantee as strong as you can afford to. The experience of many successful mail-order companies, including Sears, Land's End, and L.L. Bean, is that a 100 percent money-back guarantee at any time during the life of the product, no questions asked, works best. A tiny, tiny fraction of the people are larcenous and will try to rip you off, but the pittance you lose will be more than offset by the increased sales you make to honest folks.

Many entrepreneurs and owners of small businesses are reluctant to offer an absolute guarantee. But the few who do have discovered something very important: The strong guarantee sets them apart from the competition. That alone makes the guarantee worth it.

Structuring the Offer (Some Tips of the Trade)

The big idea in structuring your offer is to make it as compelling and irresistible as possible to the ideal prospect or customer in your target market. Here are some tips to keep in mind:

- ✓ **Create a feeling of excitement** — "let's make a deal" — so the potential buyer mentally enters into a dialogue with you.

- ✓ **Don't go over the edge into the unbelievable.** If an offer is too good to be true, it probably isn't true. Consumers are a savvy bunch. They can sniff out an insincere offer, and you'll end up being the loser.

  Instead, make sure that your offer is grounded in reality. Although there's often a strong emotional factor at play when a consumer makes a purchase, there's also a rational mind at work. People weigh very carefully the rational and the emotional in their buying decisions. Questions like "Can I afford this?" and "Can I afford it now?" and "Is this a good value?" run through the mind just as much as thoughts of "I can't live without this."

- ✓ **Make your offer relevant** — appropriate to the product and the need it fills. Would you buy it? Would your mother? Would your best friend? These factors should play just as big a part in formulating and evaluating your offer as the practical dollars-and-cents scenario of cost of goods, selling price, margin of profit, and so on.

- ✓ **Try for exclusivity.** Study the offers your competitors make; then mix and match the components of the offer to create one that you and only you can make.

- ✓ **Don't limit yourself** just to the building blocks described in the preceding section. Add a psychological element, for example. People need recognition, status, love, solace, and power. You can stimulate the psychological mainsprings of filling basic needs by appealing to fear, greed, comfort, or beauty as part of your offer. Study how your product or service appeals to the emotional needs in people and build it into your offer.

- ✓ **Finally, keep it simple** and, above all, make it easy for the customer to order.

Special considerations for fund-raisers

Fund-raising through direct mail is different from selling a product or service. Charities, religious organizations, schools, and other nonprofit groups ask for money and don't give anything tangible in return. Granted, the customer may get an inexpensive premium — a calendar or an informational pamphlet — but that's about it. So how do you structure your offer to make it compelling and irresistible?

Well, you go for a unique combination of guilt — a tug at the heartstrings — and a hint at immortality. Skillfully done, a fund-raising appeal stirs up some powerful emotions. What would you pay to be relieved of guilt? How much would you pay for immortality? Just tour a college campus or visit a church or hospital. Read the names on the buildings and on the plaques. Those people purchased a measure of immortality, perhaps as much as one can expect in this world, by giving substantial gifts. Remember this: Giving isn't selfless. It brings the giver something priceless.

Chapter 5

Identifying Your Audience

*G*ot a question for ya: What happens if you develop the best direct mail package possible and then send it to people who couldn't care less? Plain and simple, you've wasted your time and money. What you've sent is absolutely, truly junk mail.

Targeting — identifying your audience — is the best way to ensure that your prospects will find value in your direct mail product or service *and* the best way to save money as a direct mailer. By mailing fewer pieces to just the prospects who are interested in what you're selling, you save on printing, postage, and renting names.

This chapter offers approaches you can take to identify your target audience. The first thing you've got to do is take a good hard look at your current customer base — really know who your customers are. Then you can target new customers by using customer modeling or by renting mailing lists.

Knowing Your Current Customers Inside and Out

The first thing you need to do is take a very close look at your *current* customers and find out every relevant thing about them in relation to your product or service. The reason? Because other people who will want to buy your product or service are going to be similar to your current customers.

If you can develop the perfect snapshot of your current customer, finding more of them will be a lot easier.

How do you develop that perfect snapshot? You've got to talk with your customers and get as much info as you can from them. Chapter 2 covers initial research you should do to determine whether direct mail is right for you and your business. Part of that research involves phoning and surveying your customers to gather specific info about them. Check out that chapter for good questions to ask your customers.

Using Customer Modeling

Once you get as much specific info as you can about your current customers (by talking to them on the phone or sending out a survey, for example), you have options on how to use that info to zone in on your *target audience* — your prospective new customers. One option is to use *customer modeling,* which is a computer-based way of profiling your customers. This section covers the types of customer modeling that are available. (Another option is to rent mailing lists, which is covered later in this chapter.)

To get the most value out of modeling, your *house list* — the database of your own customers — should be chockfull of information about them: names, addresses, phone numbers, e-mail addresses, what they bought, when they bought it, how much they paid for it, how frequently they bought it, and any other relevant information you can capture on an order card. If your database doesn't have this kind of detailed information, start collecting it immediately (see Chapter 2). This information is a gold mine that will prove its worth many times over.

Database services

Database services enable you to submit your current list of customers and, based on the information in the database about your customers, find other prospects that have similar socioeconomic characteristics — things like where they live, the type of house they live in, the kind of cars they drive, income levels, the presence of children in the home and their ages, purchasing behavior, and much, much more. The process takes a few weeks. The analysis gives you a profile that you can use to find prospects most likely to be interested in your product or service.

Database services are available for business-to-business selling as well. The characteristics you will find for businesses include their SIC code, number of employees, sales, number and type of location, and so on.

You can find modeling database services in the directories that appear monthly in trade publications like *Target Marketing, DM News*, and *Direct Marketing Magazine*.

Regression analysis

This statistical technique is the most expensive and time consuming method of modeling. *Regression analysis* is not curling up in a fetal position on your psychiatrist's couch. It's typically used to extensively test a direct mail strategy.

To do a regression analysis, you must mail a test to a randomly selected portion of your house file or what you consider to be a good prospect file. The results of the test and whom you mailed to are analyzed to predict how many prospects will eventually buy your product. This method requires 500 to 1,000 paid orders for it to be statistically valid. If you were to get a 1 percent net response rate from your test mailing, you would have to mail 50,000 to 100,000 pieces.

Mapping

Mapping is another type of modeling that's relatively easy and quick. You analyze which zip codes or neighborhoods your customers live in. It's easy to see where the concentrations are. You can buy mapping software programs, such as Microsoft's MapPoint, that you can run on your PC. The software does the analysis automatically.

If you find that you've been mailing to areas where you have few customers, then stop. From now on, just mail to those areas where you have good market penetration — the percentage of households that are your customers.

Using Targeted Mailing Lists

Mass media — radio, television, newspapers, billboards, mass-circulation magazines, sky writing, whatever — don't offer much in the way of audience selectivity. They succeed by reaching just about *everyone*, regardless of their interests, education, occupation, gender, age, religion, hobbies — whatever characteristic you'd care to name. So advertising messages placed in these media often strive for the broadest appeals possible, hoping to interest enough people in whatever product or service is being promoted. Most of the time, it's affordable for the advertiser because the cost per thousand people reached is extremely low. A $2,000 ad in a newspaper that reaches 100,000 people, for example, costs 2/10ths of a cent per impression.

In contrast, you want your direct mail campaign to be *very* selective in terms of audience. Otherwise, you end up wasting a whole lot of money sending out a beautifully presented offer to people who just aren't interested.

Targeted mailing lists are an option to help you zone in on a selective audience. They're lists that you rent, and they contain specific info about specific people. Good mailing lists contain the names and addresses (and often other useful data) of people with common interests and buying behavior. If you can identify and describe your target audience, there's probably a mailing list you can rent to match that exact audience. Literally, thousands and thousands of mailing lists are out there.

The goal is for you to pick the right list in relation to your product or service so that you can *personally* "talk" to the people on the list — get on their wavelength, show that you recognize their interests and needs, and show and tell how your product or service will benefit them. (Check out the sidebar "Matching your product or service with the right kind of list" for some specific examples.)

Matching your product or service with the right kind of list

With thousands upon thousands of mailing lists available to rent, you're sure to find one that's just right for your product or service. Here are a few examples to help you see how:

Is your product for home decorating do-it-yourselfers? You can rent a list of people who have actually purchased home decorating books, magazines, tools, wallpaper, and so on, by mail. These people have identified their interest by their actual buying behavior.

Do you have a service to offer for owners of small businesses or home-based businesses? There are lists of mail-order buyers of similar services. And there are compiled lists of people who fit in this category.

Are you a fund-raiser for a religious or nonprofit organization who is targeting Methodist women over the age of 50 with household incomes of $35,000 and up? Yep, you can rent lists that specific — of those exact women.

Just as important as choosing the right mailing lists is avoiding the wrong lists — the ones that are too far afield or too tangential to the big benefits of your product or service. Even the most brilliant direct mail fails if you mail to the wrong lists. Smart mailers spend a lot of time and money weeding out the people who are least likely to respond.

To rent a list, you have to contact a list broker: Just look up Mailing Lists in the Yellow Pages. Or go to a business library and get a copy of the *SRDS Direct Marketing List Source*, a two-part directory published by Standard Rate and Data Service. (The Standard Rate and Data Service's phone number is 1-800-851-7737; its Web site is www.srds.com.)

List brokers help you identify which lists work best for what you're selling. Besides making suggestions, list brokers can also find out from list managers (who represent list owners) who else has been renting particular lists. If various different folks are renting the same lists over and over again, those lists are working well. (Want more info about who's who in list management? Check out the nearby sidebar about it.)

Mailing list management ("Who does what?")

Here's the lowdown on who owns what and who does what in mailing list management:

The *list owner* owns the names on a list because either those names responded to an offer that the list owner made or the owner is the actual compiler of the names. The owner decides if he/she wants to rent names to you based on the sample mail piece you submit to him/her. The owner's decision to rent is usually based on relevance to his/her customers, content, and competitive nature of what you're promoting.

The *list manager* promotes the use of the names that the list owner has put on the market. The list manager advertises the availability of the names and manages the inquiries and orders received so that the list owner can concentrate on his/her main business. The owner pays the manager.

It costs you nothing extra to use a broker. The broker is paid a commission by the list owner. (List owners gladly pay the commission because they want your business, and if you and the broker are successful, you'll likely come back for more names.)

You can rent two kinds of lists to find prospects and customers — compiled lists and response lists. The following sections take a quick look at both.

Compiled lists

Compiled lists are names of people who have been put together because of some common denominator. An example of a very broad common denominator is "all people in a certain area who have a phone." That particular compiled list is called a phone book, and, yes, you can rent names from a phone book (targeting people just by where they live).

But most compiled lists provide a lot more information. And, generally, the more information the list has that you can base your selections on, the more you pay per thousand names.

You can obtain the names of people based on things like their income level, whether they own a car or home, the types of magazines they read, their interests (gardening, stamp collecting, whatever), and on and on. You can get lists of new homeowners, recent movers, and catalog buyers by type of products and expenditure levels. The choices, they are aplenty.

Response lists

One component most compiled lists are missing is whether or not the people on the lists respond to direct mail offers. That component is often critical to your success. People who respond to direct mail will typically respond again. People who don't respond will typically continue not to respond.

Response lists are names of people who have responded previously to direct mail offers. These people typically are much more targeted to your offer, and their names cost more to rent. They typically respond better, though.

Here's a hodgepodge of tips, insights, and warnings about using response lists:

- ✔ When you rent response lists, be sure to find out what the people responded to. They may not have actually purchased something.

- ✔ The best response list is your own *house list,* the list of people who have bought from you before. If you have a new product to sell, contact these people first. If they don't want it, maybe no one will want it. (Your house list also comes into play with customer modeling, which is discussed earlier in this chapter.)

- ✔ Be selective in which names you rent. Apply what you get from customer modeling to select the best names from the files. You can usually select by gender, zip code or state, amount of purchase, how sold (mail, phone, and so on), and recency of sale.

- ✔ The best names on any file are the *Hot Line names.* These are the names of people who are new on the file within the past six months or who have purchased within the past six months or who have recently moved. Test these names first. If they don't work, chances are that the entire list won't work well for you.

If your Hot Line names test shows that this list *is* a good list for you, don't immediately rent all the rest of the names on it. Try testing another portion of the list — maybe one-fourth of it the next time. If that still works, then go for the rest. Try other selection criteria. And look for similar lists. See who's using the list you're having success with and try whatever other lists they're using.

✔ When list owners rent a list, they monitor the use of the file by including secretly encoded *seed names.* These are people who have been instructed to report the encoded mail to the list owner. The purpose of the seed names is to make sure that no one copies the list and uses it without paying for it and to make sure that no one uses it for a mailing that hasn't been approved. If you get caught doing something like that, you can end up with heavy financial consequences, and sometimes other list owners won't rent to you anymore. You can also use seed names to monitor when the mail is getting delivered.

✔ Include your own seed names in every mailing you send out. They can be the names of employees, friends, and business associates. The idea here is to keep track of *when* the mail is delivered in different parts of the country and to make sure that it *is* delivered. That way, if you get no orders from a certain area and you confirm that your seeds haven't received their mailings, you can deduce that there's a delivery problem somewhere but that the problem is not your direct mail offer itself.

Bottom line? No time invested in list research is ever wasted. Pick those names carefully and keep very good records of everything you test.

Chapter 6

Choosing Your Format

- -

In This Chapter

▶ Self-mailing formats (postcards, flyers, brochures, and such)

▶ Complete direct mail packages

- -

*T*ime to get into the details and make some choices. Are you going to mail a letter, a brochure, a post card, or maybe a full-blown direct mail package? This chapter covers various formats you can use for your direct mail piece. And it covers some reasons that you may want to choose one format over another.

As you refine your use of direct mail, you may find that different market segments need to get different formats and offers.

Postcards

Postcards are a wonderful medium for delivering a concise message that you can present clearly and completely in a small space. They're an excellent choice, for example, to let a prospect or customer know about a special event (maybe a sale) or to drive traffic to a store or Web site. Postcards offer these benefits:

✔ They're the least expensive direct mail format. They're inexpensive to produce because only one piece is being printed — no envelopes or extras.

Because postcards are inexpensive, you may be able to afford to test different offers and different creative approaches.

✔ The post office mails postcards that are no bigger than
4 ¼ x 6 inches at greatly discounted rates from first class
(less than bulk rate) and yet gives them first-class mail-
handling service.

Postcards larger than 4¼ x 6 inches have to mail at either
first-class rates or bulk rates, not postcard rates.)

✔ You can immediately attract the recipient's attention
without the person having to open an envelope.

Don't do what many postcard mailers do: They put a ter-
rific design and/or headline on the picture side of the
card and nothing but the address on the address side,
and many people never see the eye-catching design or
headline. All they see is the address side — the side
that's facing up when the mail carrier delivers it. Because
people always look at the address side of a postcard to
see whether it's for them, they may decide to throw the
card away without turning it over. That's why *both* sides
of a postcard should sell. The address side is where you
want to put your headline or attention-getting graphic.

The disadvantage of the postcard is that space is limited. You
don't have much room. You must be able to deliver a very
concise message that elicits the desired response from the
recipient: You need to gain attention, stimulate interest, provoke desire, and make the prospect take action. That's a lot
for a little postcard to accomplish. That's not to say it can't be
done; it's just more difficult. Postcards are a good way to build
awareness and stimulate interest. You've really got to hit the
nail on the head, though, to make a sale.

Watch your own mail. You probably get lots of postcards from
magazine publishers, urging you to subscribe. These postcards
are among the best being used today. Study them carefully.

Double Postcards

Double postcards are similar to regular postcards. The differences are that they're bigger (you fold them in half) and they
provide the action device that postcards are missing — a
reply card.

Thickness issues for postcards and self-mailers

For postcards up to 4¼ x 6 inches, the minimum thickness is .007 inch, or 7 millimeters. That's the minimum stock you can use to print a postcard or a double postcard (since only half of it is being returned). Any mail piece that is bigger than 4¼ x 6 inches must have a minimum thickness of .009 inch. Don't confuse thickness and weight. Weight usually doesn't matter as long as you meet the thickness requirements. (Check out Chapter 8 for more info about printing.)

The minimum thickness of a self-mailer needs to be .007 inch or .009 inch, depending on the size of the reply card that comes back to you. Also, in order for you to obtain low automated postage rates, self-mailers must be sealed. This is usually done with wafer seals or tabs, or the pieces are glued shut when the final fold is made on a folding machine. Depending on the weight of the paper you use and the relative position of the final fold to the address, you need either one or two seals. (Check out Chapters 8 and 9 for related info.)

The double postcard allows you more room to show your product, describe its benefits, get people excited about it, and get people to order it. However, it doesn't provide a means for people to pay for it.

The post office allows you to mail double postcards at the same rate as regular postcards as long as there is a reply card and as long as the double postcard is no bigger than 8½ x 6 inches and folds in half to no more than 4¼ x 6. The reply card itself doesn't have to be postage-paid, but it must be a reply card.

Self-Mailers

As their name implies, self-mailers are pieces that mail without envelopes. Technically, postcards and double postcards are self-mailers, too. But when we refer to self-mailers, we're talking about pieces that are larger and more elaborate than postcards — usually flyers and brochures that are folded so that a mailing panel is on the outside.

Printing issues for self-mailing brochures

A brochure's size can be whatever your designer comes up with, but keep in mind that most presses are designed around the 8½ x 11-inch page size. Sizes that are parts or multiples of that size print more efficiently (11 x 17, 17 x 22, or 5½ x 8½ for example). Ask your printer which sizes work best with the equipment he or she has or find a printer who has equipment that will efficiently print the size you created.

If your brochure has a lot of dark ink on it, ask the printer to varnish it. Varnishing puts a protective coating over the ink and helps prevent smudges and fingerprints from being seen.

When you fold the brochure, ask the printer to score the folds. Doing so breaks the fibers in the paper so that you don't see a jagged edge on the fold, which is caused from the coating lifting off of the paper. It's most noticeable when there's a lot of ink across the fold because you see the white paper through the crack. Uncoated paper has the same problem, but it's usually not as noticeable because there's no coating and usually less ink.

Many people believe that self-mailers don't work as well as mail in an envelope. They say that self-mailers scream "direct mail" and that many recipients immediately toss them into the trash without opening them. However, one category where self-mailers work consistently well is seminar and conference promotions. If you're a member of any large professional organization, you probably receive such self-mailers often. Save and study them, and you'll see that nearly all of them follow the same tactics in terms of copy.

Self-mailers are relatively inexpensive to mail because, just like postcards, there are no envelope and lettershop inserting costs. Typically, though, response rates from self-mailers aren't as good as those you get from envelope mailings. But because the production costs are less, they can still be more profitable. It depends, of course, on what you're selling and how much money you earn from a sale.

Booklets and Catalogs

As you know from your mailbox, a lot of direct mail is catalogs and booklets. Booklets are informative, and catalogs sell products. Both are produced the same way. If you have a lot of information to impart or many products to sell, you would use this format. Booklets and catalogs are produced like books, and the production methods are beyond the scope of this chapter. A good source of information is International Paper Company's *Pocket Pal*.

Talk to your printer early in the planning process to find out the most economical formats. And make an actual-size blank sample (called a *dummy),* staples and all, on the same paper stock you'll use (see Chapter 8 for more info on printing and paper stock). Get your lettershop or post office to weigh it (your printer can calculate how much the ink will weigh) and verify that it's addressable and mailable at the best rate. (Chapter 9 covers info about lettershops and post offices and delivering your direct mail piece.)

Complete Direct Mail Packages

When you have a whole story to tell, nothing is more effective than the traditional direct mail package. It gives you all the room you need to tell your story. It can generate a lot of excitement. It can show your product or allow you to fully illustrate your service. It can *sell.*

The typical direct mail package (assuming there is such a thing) includes several components: an envelope, a letter, a brochure, an order form with a reply device, and some extras (stuff like buck slips, lift letters, stickers, and so on). This section goes through the typical components and some things you need to consider about them.

In every component of your direct mail except the envelope, ask for the order in some way. And be sure that every component includes your address and phone number at least. Make responding to your offer easy.

Envelope printing and mailing considerations

Paper for envelopes is usually wove or coated. Use coated paper when you want to print four-color process on the envelope and want a glossy look. Usually, people use 70# text that's coated on one side. The inside isn't coated so that the paper goes through the converting equipment without too much shifting around. (Chapter 8 covers printing matters in detail.)

If you want the best postage rates, you have to automate your mail (a topic that's covered in Chapter 9). One of the requirements for receiving automated rates is that your mail be pre-bar coded. If you use a window envelope, the bar code has to show through the window. Placement of the address and the size of the window become critical. Not only must the entire bar code show through the window, but it must also be completely visible when someone taps the envelope to either side or to the bottom. The postal service calls this the *Tap Test*. If you fail the Tap Test, your postage is greatly increased.

The envelope

The first thing people see is the envelope. So it must grab people's attention and stimulate a desire to open it. You can accomplish this with an effective headline, or you can leave the envelope entirely blank to create curiosity. Which tactic works better? Well, that depends on how good the copy on your envelope is, what you're selling, and who you're selling to. It's one of those things you have to test.

 If your mailing uses a 6 x 9-inch envelope, you probably want to put copy on it. That's a commercial envelope — people don't use it for personal mail. Like a flyer, its size announces that it's direct mail, and many people won't open it unless you give them a compelling reason to do so.

A major consideration for the envelope is whether it'll have a window. If you use a window, the address of the recipient must show through it. Usually, the address is on the top of the letter or on the reply device (usually an order form). If you don't use a window and the name and/or address is also on the inside of the envelope, you have to do a *matched mailing*. Obviously, you want the same name on the inside and outside. Commercial lettershops charge a premium for matched mailings.

You can send out a mailing without the name and address on something inside the envelope. If you're mailing multiple lists at the same time, however, and want to measure the responsiveness of a list, you must code the piece that comes back to you. (A *code* is a way for you to recognize what list and/or offer was mailed to this particular person. It can be as simple as an *A, B,* or *C.*) If the reply device is not coded for list and offer and creative tests, you lose very valuable information.

The letter

The letter is the most important part of the direct mail package. It is where you get to tell your story — do all your selling. The letter is what makes direct mail personal. You have to make the letter interesting so that it draws the reader into your story.

Sheets versus pages: There is a difference

We want to clarify a little paper terminology here because there's often some confusion about it. Each piece of paper is called a *sheet.* Each side of a sheet of paper that a letter is printed on, as in a book, is called a *page.* If you use both sides of one sheet of paper, the letter is two pages long. If you use one side each of two sheets of paper, the letter is still two pages long but on two sheets of paper. Which, of course, is more expensive because you're using twice as much paper. Doing it that way may be worth it, though, if you want your mail to have a more formal or elegant appeal. Test it.

Which way you decide to produce the letter is a function of how formal the letter should look and how big your budget is. If you print on both sides of a sheet of paper, be sure that your paper has enough opacity so that the text on the other side doesn't show through. Usually, the heavier the paper is, the more opacity it has. But remember: The heavier it is, the more it costs (you pay by the pound). To overcome the opacity problem, paper mills produce papers that have high opacity at lower weights. Examples are Finch Opaque and Cougar Opaque.

Writing a good letter is an art that's learned over many years. That's why some copywriters get paid thousands of dollars for writing the letter. In Chapter 7, we tell you some tricks of the trade so you can write great letters, too.

Your package may not need more than a letter (and a reply device) because the letter can contain all the elements you need to make your sales effort successful (gain attention, stimulate interest, provoke desire, and get action). The letter can be as long as it needs to be to accomplish your goal.

The brochure

The brochure shows that your product is real by displaying it, usually in full color. Everyone knows that a picture is worth a thousand words. Well, here's where you show your pictures. A brochure should also include headlines that re-tell and re-sell the benefits mentioned in the letter. Repetitious? Yes. But repetition sells.

Tell 'em what you're gonna tell 'em. Then tell 'em. And then tell 'em you told 'em. It's an old technique in selling. Follow it.

Picture captions are another important element to include in your brochure. Tests by the legendary advertising man David Ogilvy showed that often the first thing people actually read attentively in a brochure are the picture captions. So put your strongest benefits in the captions.

People buy benefits. Although your brochure shows the product's features, make sure that your copy describes how those features are *benefits* to the buyer. The fact that a car has a 300-horsepower engine is not what's important. What's important is that you can quickly accelerate onto a highway and pass other cars safely. If you can dramatize that benefit with a headline, a picture, and a caption, you move closer to making the sale.

If you're selling a service, the brochure is often used to further describe the service. Insurance mailings may include a rate chart. Second mortgage companies often enclose a question-and-answer brochure to further explain their product. These types of brochures don't need to be in full color. Effective use of second colors and shadings can be just as effective at a lower cost.

The order form with a reply device

The order form serves several purposes, and it must be able to stand on its own. When you write and design the order form, pretend that the recipient has thrown everything away except it. So make sure it contains

- The offer
- The terms of the offer
- How to respond
- The benefits of what you're selling
- The guarantee

On the order form, fill in the recipient's name and address as it appears on your mailing list or house file. Ask the recipient to make any necessary corrections. Since you're "pre-populating" the form (that is, filling in the information already), this is often used as the addressing vehicle that shows through the window of the envelope.

Envelope considerations for the reply device

In order to be machine-inserted into an outer envelope, the reply device (or anything else) should be at least ½-inch narrower than the envelope. You don't want to make it too much narrower, though, or you'll have problems with the Tap Test (see the sidebar "Envelope printing and mailing considerations" for info about the Tap Test). The reply envelope needs the same ½ inch to fit into the outer envelope.

So if the reply form and the reply envelope are the same ½-inch narrower, how do you fit the reply device into the reply envelope? Put a perforation onto the reply device so that the recipient makes the width narrower before putting it into the envelope. You can encourage the recipient to do so with a printed perforation and by putting things like receipts or guarantees on the stub you want torn off and kept.

Printing tidbits about buck slips

Buck slips can be printed on both coated and uncoated paper depending on the graphics. If you want to show an extra gift that you get if you "order now," you may want to use coated paper. If you're giving a discount certificate, uncoated paper will probably work just fine. Same with the number of ink colors you use: If you want to show a gift, you probably want to go with four colors to show it off properly. A certificate will probably look great in, say, just green and black.

For the reply device, many options are available: an address, a phone number, a fax number, an e-mail or Internet address, or a business reply card. Don't include all of them, though. You don't want to provide too many options.

Unless you're mailing to a very tech-savvy list of people, don't send the recipients to a Web site to reply to an offer that you send in the mail. On their way to your Web site, there are too many obstacles and distractions for them.

Other stuff

You may want to add extra components to your direct mail package to call attention to special offers, emphasize other benefits to the user, or involve the user with the package.

- ✔ **Buck slips and flyers:** Use buck slips and flyers to further describe your product and its benefits or to enhance your offer. For example, you may print a buck slip or flyer to describe a special offer that you get "if you act quickly." (Buck slips, by the way, got their name because they're the same or similar size as dollar bills.)

- ✔ **Stickers:** Stickers are typically used to involve the recipient with the direct mail package. You want to get the recipient to more closely read the contents of your package so that he or she knows what to do with the stickers. Yes/No option stickers, stamps, and such make the recipient take an action and lead him or her toward the ultimate yes. The goal is to have the recipient put the sticker on the part of the order form that is sent back.

You may be wondering why a No sticker is used. It emphasizes the Yes. People have tested their mailings and found that a No sticker increases the number of orders they get.

✔ **Lift letters:** Lift letters are extra little notes (often folded like personal notes) that are put in the package to lift response — an endorsement from a third party, for example. Publishers use lift letters to sell subscriptions. The editor of the magazine may write the main letter in the package, but the publisher or perhaps a celebrity signs the lift letter.

Make sure that the lift letter is signed by a different person from the one who signed the main letter. Since it's a miniletter, uncoated paper works just fine.

✔ **Magalogs:** Magalogs are combination magazines and catalogs. They're minimagazines. They show some of the editorial content of the real magazine or newsletter and have a built-in response device. They give the recipient a feel for what the actual product will be like.

A special consideration for business-to-business sellers

Business-to-business mailers have a unique problem that business-to-consumer mailers don't: how to get past the gatekeeper — the person who screens the mail for your prospect. You can get past the gatekeeper by sending very personal looking mail or by sending dimensional packages.

A *dimensional package* is usually a box or maybe a tube. It really stands out on the desk from the other mail and looks very important. It's difficult for the gatekeeper to keep this kind of package from the recipient.

Mailing a dimensional package can be expensive. The packaging is certainly more expensive than an envelope, and it typically needs to be hand-assembled. In the business-to-business world, though, a sale can be worth hundreds or thousands of dollars. One sale can pay for a lot of direct mail packages. A dimensional package can well be worthwhile.

Chapter 7

Creating Your Work of Art

● ●

In This Chapter

▶ Deciding whether to use a freelancer

▶ Writing copy that sells

▶ Designing an attractive mail-order piece

● ●

*B*eing a handyman around your house can save you a ton of money . . . if you know what you're doing. Writing and designing your direct mail piece is no different than repairing your home. Do it right, and you're pocketing extra change. Do it wrong, and you may as well be throwing your money into the gutter.

In this chapter, we tell you why you may want to hire a freelancer to write and design your direct mail piece. And if you're a true do-it-yourselfer, we even give you tips on how to make your text and design the best that it can be.

Finding a Freelancer (and Why You Probably Should)

Many budding entrepreneurs are tempted to write and design their direct mail piece unaided. It seems easy, and doing so can save you money and be fun at the same time. You may very well be thinking, "Okay, how hard can it be to type a few words about my product and place them on a piece of paper?" Actually, writing text that sells is probably harder than you think. Unless you're a writer and designer by trade (and you're probably not both), you should hire a professional with a proven track record to handle one or both parts of this project.

Generally, you'll need two freelancers: one to write the copy, and the other to create the design (although you may be lucky enough to find someone who can do both well). To find freelancers, check with local direct marketing clubs, the Direct Marketing Association in New York (212-768-7277), or your local yellow pages.

You can expect to pay about $2,000 to $3,000 each for a good freelance direct mail writer or designer who gives you an envelope, letter, brochure, and order card. You may even pay $5,000 to $10,000. And believe it or not, some writers and designers receive $15,000 to $20,000 and up from their top clients. Whether your business budget falls on the lower or higher end of this scale, though, the following sections can help you find a freelancer to meet your needs.

Whether you write your own copy or hire outside talent, *you* are the person who decides on the final form of the direct mail.

The copy

Even though you can write high school and college essays, e-mails, business letters, and memos, you still may not have what it takes to be a direct mail writer. Writing direct mail copy that *sells* is a subtle art, one that requires a lot of experience. Here's what you should look for in a writer:

- ✔ He or she should have experience in *direct mail writing* — say at least five years' worth, preferably more.

- ✔ He or she should have a portfolio that has many samples of actual direct mail that other companies have mailed. Ask which of the samples are controls and ask for references to confirm that.

The design

Some people have a knack for design, and, well, frankly, some people don't. Graphic design requires real artistic talent, training, and experience. If you didn't do well in art class, then you definitely aren't a candidate for designing your own mailer. Here are some tips to help you find a good designer:

- ✔ He or she should have experience in *direct mail design* — say at least five years' worth, preferably more.

- ✔ He or she should have a portfolio that has many samples of actual direct mail that other companies have mailed. Ask which of the samples are controls and ask for references to confirm that.

- ✔ He or she should know how to use desktop publishing programs.

Writers and designers often work in teams. If you see samples from a writer that you like a lot, ask her to recommend designers.

Forget about doing the graphic design yourself unless your direct mail will consist solely of a plain envelope, a letter, and a plain order form. If you want to design anything more sophisticated (and you probably do), then you need to hire a freelance designer.

If you're really convinced that you have the talent for design, skip to the section "If You're a Design Whiz . . .," later in this chapter.

Ask yourself the right questions

One of the things you can do if you're having trouble writing is to visualize your audience. Don't worry. It's not as hard as it sounds.

- ✔ Imagine your reader. Is she a stay-at-home mom or a Type-A executive? Is he a music lover or a hockey fan?

- ✔ Ask yourself all sorts of questions about exactly *who* your prospect is — and how your product can fulfill his or her needs, hopes, and desires.

- ✔ Write an imaginary mini-biography about this person. What does

he look like? How old is he? Did he go to college? Graduate school? What does he do for a living? You can even thumb through magazines and look for a picture of someone whom you visualize to be your ideal prospect. Tear out the picture, tape your mini-biography to it, and pin it up where you can glance at it from time to time as you write.

Now, when you write, "talk" to this person in a personal, friendly way that sells.

If You're a Wordsmith . . .

Strong copy and design separate the winners from the losers in direct mail. And no matter how strong a writer you are, if you're convinced that you can write your own direct mail piece, you can benefit from the direct mail writing tips in the following sections.

Make the copy personal

The tone of your copy, especially the sales letter, should sound as if it's coming from a good friend. This friendly person uses words to demonstrate that he or she cares about the needs, hopes, and desires of the reader. Follow these tips for creating friendly, personal copy:

- ✔ **Smile, smile, smile!** When you smile when you write, your text automatically sounds friendlier. (Really.) We know an excellent freelance copy writer who keeps a mirror in front of her so that she can keep an eye on her facial expressions as she writes. Smiling helps her keep her mood friendly and upbeat — and that translates into warm, friendly, caring words that smile on the page and make people want to read more.

- ✔ **Visualize your client or customer.** If you're struggling to get words on paper, visualize your prospect, customer, or client. Sure, you're writing to a thousand or a million people, but your approach must be to sell them *one at a time!* The sidebar "Ask yourself the right questions" tells you how to "create" the customer your direct mail piece targets.

Focus on benefits, not features

Features are nice, yes. They give you the lowdown on your product or service — the straight facts. But benefits make the difference. When you write about benefits, you're transforming the meaningless laundry lists of facts into warm fuzzy feelings.

In the window of Macy's on 34th Street in New York City, we saw a beautiful display of stainless steel cookware. The only sign in the display said "Triple Ply." We don't know about you, but those words didn't tell us much. (Okay, so we're not experienced cooks or metallurgists.) Triple Ply is merely a feature. The display would have been far more successful if it told us what triple ply was, how it would benefit us, and if it would make our dinners taste better.

Figure 7-1 gives you an example of a sales letter that speaks features (we've changed a few details to protect the guilty).

Dear Executive:

We are pleased to enclose information about the A-2000 Model Snurfenborg, now available for lease. The wide range of speeds, capacity, and gauge of alloys processed by the A-2000 is designed to meet your needs and are supported by a truly dedicated technical and administrative group with lease plans available through our parent company, Snurfenborg Holdings.

The essence of Snurfenborg is embodied in our philosophy: quality and productivity. Constant dedication to this philosophy allows us to design and build the A-2000 with conveniences found only on Snurfenborg machines. The quality we build into every Snurfenborg assures the high residual value your business demands in leased alloy processing equipment.

This package provides you with the information on our exciting A-2000 Model, directions on how to contact our lease department, available incentives, lease/finance options, and answers to questions you may have about the Snurfenborg Lease Program.

Please contact us, and together with Snurfenborg Lease and Remarketing Operations, we will demonstrate our ability to help you meet your alloy processing needs.

Sincerely,

Sully Snurfenborg, President

Figure 7-1: Features, features, features — boring.

The letter in Figure 7-1 is one of the worst sales letters we have ever seen because it only talks about features. And who cares? Readers want to know how this product benefits them, not that it has a "high residual value." To speak benefits, you should say something like,

The quality we build into every Snurfenborg assures you of high residual value at the end of your lease — real savings that lower your leasing costs! That means higher bottom line profits from every Snurfenborg machine.

Lower costs. Higher profits. Ah, *benefits* to warm the heart of the steeliest executive! Now *that's* warm and fuzzy!

Motivate your reader to action

Not everyone who receives your letter is in the "buying window" for your product or service. But if you've done your targeting properly, all your readers will at least be interested (see Chapter 5). Your letter must motivate your *prime prospects* (those ready to buy) to ask you for more information.

- **Personalize your letter.** Don't use the phrase "Dear Executive" or something as impersonal as "Dear Sir or Madam." Although personalizing your letter may cost a little more, doing so shows that you care enough to know the name of the person you're writing to. You can't always personalize your letters, but try to do so when you can.

- **Get the reader involved.** Don't ever start the letter with "We" or "I." The reader doesn't know you, so why should he or she care about you? Instead, use "you" so that the letter is about the reader right from the get-go.

- **Present the benefit and then get into the information.** Readers care about information only if you've already presented them with a benefit that makes them curious for information.

✔ **Say how features benefit the reader.** Readers don't care about the features "Wide range of speeds, capacity, and gauge." But tell them how these features benefit them, and you'll make them happy. For example,

The A-2000 gives you flexibility. You can choose from 7 speeds to match any make of spot-welding equipment in your plant. Its 100-ton capacity means you can run all day at high speed without ever shutting down to replenish feedstock. You'll meet your most demanding production schedules with ease. And you can run any gauge alloy from .0001" standard sheets to solid 6" x 6" bars with one simple lever adjustment.

✔ **Use everyday language.** "Essence of . . . philosophy" (refer to paragraph two of Figure 7-1) is a real yawner.

✔ **Make your brochures obvious.** If the mailing includes a brochure, it should be obvious. But if you feel a compelling need to tell the reader about your brochure, say something like,

Right now, take a look at the enclosed brochure that describes how the A-2000 can go to work for you in as little as two weeks. And use the Comparative Rate Chart to see how affordable your lease can be.

✔ **Ask for the order.** In Figure 7-1, the writer didn't ask for the order! Yes, he did say "Please contact us," but that's wimpy. Here's a way to make the request much stronger, more personal, and much more likely to get results.

Please call me. My direct line is toll-free 800-555-5555. You'll get prompt answers to any questions about the A-2000 and a free, no-obligation rate quote on your lease in less than five minutes.

Use *call* instead of *contact.* You want your reader to get in touch with you, but "Please contact us" is way too impersonal. *Call* is more direct and action-oriented. Also, If you include everything in your direct mail package like you're supposed to, your reader doesn't need to get in touch with you via a phone call. She should be able to just send back a reply card.

✔ **Say why the reader should lease rather than buy (or vice versa).** If you want your reader to lease something, you need to tell them about the benefits. Otherwise, he'll just ask, "Why shouldn't I just purchase this product?" In Figure 7-1, for example, the writer should have mentioned cash or credit availability and tax considerations.

✔ **Don't overlook the P.S. in your letter!** The postscript is one of the most important parts of the letter. In a letter to your mom, the P.S. is most likely to be an afterthought, something you forgot to mention in the main part of the letter. In a sales letter, the P.S. is a powerful sales tool.

Tests have proven that people who read direct mail sales letters don't start by actually "reading" the letter; they skim it quickly. And the first thing they actually *read* is the P.S. Mention your biggest benefit. And then hook the reader with something like, "FREE GIFT when you order within 10 days!" (And don't tell what the free gift is.)

Keep in mind that a direct mail campaign is like a boxing match: You won't be able to get the close (or the knock-out) with just one punch. So the letter that you're sending needs to generate *action* from your readers.

Structure your letter correctly

Long sentences, sentence fragments, poor grammar — all are big no-no's when it comes to direct mail writing (or any kind of writing for that matter).

Sentence and paragraph length

Long sentences force your reader to struggle to remember the beginning of the sentence. That's work, not fun. Reading your letter should be fun. Make sure that you write short sentences.

The same holds true for paragraphs — keep 'em short. Not only do short paragraphs make the letter easier to read, but they open up the layout of the letter as well. With an open layout, your letter looks like a quick, easy read and not something that's difficult and ponderous. Compare Figures 7-2 and 7-3.

In sales letters, whether to business prospects or consumers, don't make any paragraph more than five lines long — count 'em: *five!*

Grammar

Correct grammar is also important. Of course, you can always break the rules if you have a good sense of your target audience. But you need to *know* the rules to break them.

Before you publish anything, proofread it, but *don't* proofread right after you write. You'll be sure to miss something. Instead, set the material aside for a day (or more if you can) and *then* go back over it. Better yet, have someone else proofread it for you. Here's another little tip for those of you who create your work on a computer: Proofread a printed version. For some reason, catching spelling and grammar mistakes is easier on a hardcopy.

Dear Executive:

We are pleased to enclose information about the A-2000 Model Snurfenborg, now available for lease. The wide range of speeds, gauge of alloys, and capacity processed by the A-2000 is designed to meet your needs and are supported by a truly dedicated technical and administrative group with lease plans available through our parent company, Snurfenborg Holdings.

The essence of Snurfenborg is embodied in our philosophy: Quality and Productivity. Constant dedication to this philosophy allows us to design and build the A-2000 with conveniences found only on Snurfenborg machines. The Quality we build into every Snurfenborg assures the high residual value your business demands in leased alloy processing equipment.

This package provides you with the information on our exciting A-2000 Model, directions on how to contact our lease department, available incentives, lease/finance options, and answers to questions you may have about the Snurfenborg Lease Program. Please contact us, and together with Snurfenborg Lease and Remarketing Operations, we will demonstrate our ability to help you meet your alloy processing needs.

Sincerely,
Sully Snurfenborg, President

Figure 7-2: This letter's text is dense to look at and read.

Dear Executive:

We are pleased to enclose information about the A-2000 Model Snurfenborg, now available for lease.

The wide range of speeds, gauge of alloys, and capacity processed by the A-2000 is designed to meet your needs and are supported by a truly dedicated technical and administrative group with lease plans available through our parent company, Snurfenborg Holdings.

The essence of Snurfenborg is embodied in our philosophy:

Quality and Productivity.

Constant dedication to this philosophy allows us to design and build the A-2000 with conveniences found only on Snurfenborg machines.

The Quality we build into every Snurfenborg assures the HIGH RESIDUAL VALUE your business demands in leased alloy processing equipment.

This package provides you with the information on our exciting A-2000 Model, directions on how to

- Contact our lease department,
- Available incentives,
- Lease/finance options, and
- Answers to questions you may have about the Snurfenborg Lease Program.

Please contact us, and together with Snurfenborg Lease and Remarketing Operations, we will demonstrate our ability to help you meet your alloy processing needs.

Sincerely,
Sully Snurfenborg, President

Figure 7-3: The open design of this letter makes it much easier to read.

Choose your words carefully

Correct grammar and short sentences and paragraphs won't make the sale for you. The words do. Be certain to use *power words* and to be specific.

Use power words

Power words make your readers think of images, tastes, flavors, smells, touches, and sounds. They stimulate your readers' senses, emotions, and imagination. Try these words on for size and use them every time you get the chance:

You	Save
Free	Exclusive
New	Special
Secret	Satisfy
Discover	Misunderstood (this one makes people curious)
Good news	Limited time offer
Sale	

Be specific

Be specific when you write your copy. Use words that describe the end-user benefits of your product or service exactly. If you're trying to sell a toaster to someone who's never seen or used a toaster before, for example, don't launch into a description of mechanical and electrical parts. Instead, use something like this:

Imagine taking an ordinary piece of bread and in just one minute heating it and toasting it to a golden brown. As it toasts, your kitchen will be filled with the aroma of baking bread. And when you take your first bite, you'll be amazed at how the ordinary taste of plain bread has been transformed into a delicious nut-like flavor.

 Whenever possible, use specific numbers to support benefits. Numbers are real and indisputable and add to believability. And when you talk about savings, be specific with exact amounts. "Save $32.50" is better than "Half off" or "Save 50%." Don't make your reader do mental math. "Half" and "50%" are abstract. The amount "$32.50" is concrete, real money you can put in your pocket.

Make it as long as it needs to be

Don't worry about your letter's length. In test after test, in every category of business-to-business or consumer direct mail, long letters have proven to sell more than short letters. So write away! Your sales letter should be long enough to close the sale — no more, no less. You need to cover the list of reasons your readers will buy in order of priority, extol each reason, and then fully explain all the benefits. Only then should you end your letter.

Don't omit any reason. The first two, three, or seven reasons may not close the sale, but for some people, the eighth or ninth reasons do. If you stop after the fifth reason when there are eight reasons your product or service is great, you could very well lose some of your prospects.

If you're writing copy for a postcard, you do have space limitations. In that case, you need to choose your words carefully. Make every word count. State your benefits in the headline (yes, you want a headline — it attracts attention). Make sure that you give your readers all the necessary facts, including places, times, prices, phone numbers, addresses, and whatever you are communicating. And oh yeah — don't forget to cover the benefits!

If you have the space, say it with pictures

A *self-mailer* combines a brochure and a letter in one piece, so you can even add pictures to your letter to spice it up. Your pictures need to illustrate what you're describing with your text. If your text and pictures don't work together, you'll lose the reader's attention as he tries to find the illustration that goes with your words.

And, of course, you also have to include the benefits. Put them in your headlines and subheads. Include your phone number, Web address, and, if you have a coupon to order from, don't forget the code so that you can track your response.

If You're a Design Whiz . . .

We highly advise you to hire a professional. Not only is design hard to master, but if your product or service is "your baby," you will have a hard time being objective. But if you have artistic talent, you may decide to draw up your direct mail piece's basic design yourself.

Design is not just about photos or illustrations. It's the overall layout. Good graphic design draws the reader in, guides her through the copy, and focuses her attention on key benefits. Above all, good direct mail design organizes all the copy and graphic elements to move the sales story forward, right to the order form, toll-free phone number, or whatever.

If you design your own mail piece, be sure to show it to friends and associates to get their reactions. Ask for honest opinions and suggestions and make sure that you listen.

Using color

You may be tempted to use color because, well, color is pretty. If you can, why shouldn't you? Actually, color — whether you use it and *how* you use it — is a major design element. If you're not careful, your piece may end up looking like it spent the afternoon in the hands of a five year old with a box of crayons. Here are some things to think about:

- ✔ **Will color help you sell your product or service?** For certain products, such as food, fashions, and jewelry, the answer is yes. But keep in mind that zillions of newspaper ads and mail-order catalogs appear in black and white.

- ✔ **Can you afford it?** Color adds cost to your design.

- ✔ **Where would color be most effective?** In a good two-color letter or brochure, color can help draw the eye, so use it to punch up the important stuff. Headlines and subheads should be in color.

If you decide to use color, you can use it in specific ways for maximum effect:

- ✔ Underline key words in color.

- ✔ Use yellow highlighting to make certain words pop out. Tests reported by the DMA show that yellow highlighting helps close the sale.

- ✔ If you place a message in the margins of your letter in handscript, do it in color. Blue is good, and so is red.

Choosing a font

You want your text to be easy to read. What font you choose has a big impact on readability.

- ✔ **Serif type.** These fonts have little tails hanging off the ends of the letters. Serif fonts are easier to read.

- ✔ **Sans serif type.** Sans serif fonts have no tails, and they're harder to read in small type, although they're often used for things like headlines.

- ✔ **Reverse type.** Reverse type is white letters in a background color. It's also more difficult to read.

- ✔ *Italic text.* Although good when used to emphasize important words or phrases, italic text is difficult to read when it's used for long paragraphs.

The font size also affects how readable your direct mail is. Whenever you can, use a type size of at least 10 points.

Don't mix too many typestyles and sizes; otherwise, you're direct mail letter will look more like a ransom note pasted together with words cut from various magazines.

Using a word-processing program for direct mail layout

You can easily lay out a letter by using the word-processing programs available today. You can adjust the margins, select the size and style of type you want, add italics, bold face, and underline, center headlines, and change paragraph indents left and right. But just because you *can* make these changes so easily, doesn't mean you *should.* Here are some principles to follow when you lay out your sales letters.

- ✔ **Use the standard letterhead paper your business has on hand.** This makes setting the left and right margins of your letter easy. Just be sure to use ample margins.

- ✔ **Consider including a *Johnson box* at the top of your letterhead.** This headline-like type is usually several lines long, appears in bold type, is centered, and sometimes has a box rule around it. Johnson box headlines are enthusiastic in tone and manner. They state the Big Benefit, make an offer, get you excited, and make you want to read more.

- ✔ **Don't be cutesy.** After the Johnson box, simply follow the expected format of a letter. Being cutesy distracts most readers.

- ✔ **End a one-page letter the usual way.** A "Sincerely," followed by the letter signer's signature, typed name, and title works nicely. Don't forget to add room for a signature.

- ✔ **If your letter is longer than one page, write "Over, please" or "Please continue" in the lower right corner.** This tip may seem obvious, of course, but when you *tell* people what to do, they tend to do it.

- ✔ ***Never* end page one of a multipage letter with a complete sentence or a complete idea.** End page one with a *cliffhanger,* something intriguing that induces your reader to turn the page:

  Another profitable benefit you get from the A-2000 is

  Over, please . . .

- ✔ **Don't forget the P.S. on a multipage letter.** On a multipage letter, the reader skims to the bottom of the first page, sees the cliffhanger, and *turns the page!* Pow! You deliver another benefit, and your prospect is hooked. He goes back and reads the whole letter.

Chapter 8

Printing Your Offer

● ●

In This Chapter

▶ Getting your direct mail piece ready for print

▶ Choosing your paper and ink

▶ Understanding the different types of presses

● ●

*O*nce you're happy with the copy and design of your direct mail piece (see Chapter 7), you may feel ready to shout, "Roll the presses!" But you can't just hand over your work of art to a printer; you still have some work ahead of you. In this chapter, we tell you how to prepare your creation for print, how to decide on the perfect paper and ink, and how to determine which press is right for you.

Mastering the Prepress Process: Desktop Publishing

Today, almost all *prepress* work (everything that's done before your work goes to the press) is done on computers using page layout programs, such as Quark or PageMaker. Using these desktop publishing programs, you can generate proofs of your creations and double-check them. And once you're happy with your results, you can even send them to a printer via disks or the Internet, and you never have to leave the comforts of your office.

Why should you spend valuable time using a desktop publishing program? Because you save time. With a desktop publishing program, you can work more efficiently and quickly, and making changes later, if you have to, is much easier. You can also easily add special effects and indicate where you will use colors. Programs like Microsoft Word offer many of the same features and are also easy to use.

What's all that gobbledygook at the end of my filename?

Once you start playing around with graphic files and page layout programs, you'll probably notice that the files have weird extensions. Unlike .doc, which indicates a Word document, these file extensions aren't always intuitive.

Most files, however, are saved using a page description language called *Postscript*. You also see the file extensions JPG and TIF files, which are used for graphics. Text files are saved in any number of file formats.

PDF (Portable Document Format) creates perfect Postscript files that are compatible with other operating systems, fonts, and platforms. This portability makes PDFs extremely popular in the graphics art world. PDF has also become a de facto standard for storing documents on the Web.

If you work with a graphic designer, these terms might come up. If you work on your own, you may never need to know this stuff.

Choosing a Printing Service

Nearly every city and town in the U.S. has printing companies. How do you know which one to use?

- ✔ **Find one that's familiar with printing direct mail pieces.** There are so many things to look out for when you produce direct mail that using a printer who is familiar with the process automatically gives you extra eyes to help make sure you didn't make a mistake.

- ✔ **Ask to see a sample of their work.** Ask specifically to see samples of direct mail pieces.

- ✔ **Find out what you'll be charged to print your pieces.** Give the printer all the specifications for the job (provide a sample, if you can) and be as specific as possible. Figure 8-1 shows a sample quote request that you can use as a guide. Give the same specifications to two or three different printers who have shown you samples you like. If they can all meet your schedule, choose the printer who offers the best price or the one you'll feel most comfortable working with.

```
                    HORAH GRAPHICS INC
                 49 W. 37TH ST, 13TH FLOOR
                    NEW YORK, NY 10018
212-921-4521                            FAX 212-921-4831

                    REQUEST FOR QUOTE

PLEASE SUBMIT THIS FORM WITH YOUR PRICING ON IT.  PLEASE
QUOTE ANY ALTERNATIVES THAT WOULD BE ECONOMICAL AND STILL
MAKE SENSE.

JULY 10, 2000

DATE QUOTE NEEDED: JULY 15, 2000

FROM: Dick Goldsmith

TO: Wilson Press

ITEM: Brochure for Dime Mailing

FLAT SIZE: 11" X 17" plus bleed

FOLDED SIZE: 5-1/2" X 8-1/2"

STOCK: 70# Coated 2 sides Grade 3

COLORS: 4/4 process

BLEEDS: Yes

INK COVERAGE: Medium

FOLDS: 2

QUANTITY: 50,000

ART SUPPLIED:  Disk

F.O.B.: Dock

OTHER: 1 vertical perforation and 1 horizontal perf
```

Figure 8-1: A sample quote request. Be as specific as you can.

Deciding on Paper and Ink

Once you're ready to print your direct mail piece, you don't just walk in to a printer, hand them your creation, and say, "Hey, can you print this?" Or at least you shouldn't without asking about paper and ink.

Discuss paper, ink, and color choices with your printer as early in the design stage as possible. Show him or her what you're planning and ask whether it's the most economical way to proceed. You can save a lot of money this way.

What type of paper do you want?

The paper you select greatly affects the look of your final printed piece. Like just about everything else in life, the more you spend, the better the quality of your final product.

- ✔ If you're going to print a brochure with pictures, you probably want to use a gloss or matte coated paper. The ink will look real shiny and more lifelike.

- ✔ For letters, use uncoated paper so that the type on the letter can be read easily, without the glare you sometimes get from coated paper.

- ✔ If you plan to print on both sides of the paper, make sure the paper you select has enough opacity so that what's printed on the backside doesn't show through. (Show through can be very distracting to the reader.)

- ✔ If you're printing a reply card (or any card to be sent in the mail) that's 6" x 4 ¼" or less, the paper must be .007" thick. If the card is larger, the minimum thickness for a mailing piece is .009". Your printer and designer can help.

The two most common types of paper used in direct mail are wove and text. What makes *text paper* different from *wove paper* is how the fibers of the paper are interwoven when the paper is manufactured. *Bond paper* is also similar in appearance to wove, but it often contains some percentage of cotton or other cloth. Bond papers, while used for stationery, are not generally used for direct mail because of the expense. You can get a great variety of textured surface text papers that look like bond but don't cost as much. Table 8-2 can help you figure out what kind of paper to use for what.

Table 8-2	Paper and Its Uses
Type of Paper	*What's Commonly Printed on It*
Wove	Envelopes
Bond	Stationery
Coated text paper	Glossy brochures, cards, magazines, and catalogs
Uncoated text paper	Letters, lift letters, brochures, and cards

Uncoated text paper can come with different finishes like linen, basket weave, and laid. In addition, many colors are available, starting with white and running the gamut of the rainbow. Wove papers are also available in different colors, though not to the extent that text papers are.

 If you print four-color process (see the section "What about ink?" for details) on uncoated or textured paper, you need to make sure that it's done right. Since most printers use coated papers for four color process, it requires special techniques to make the inks look good on uncoated papers. Ask your printer to show you samples of his/her work.

What about paper weight?

The weight of the papers you use is important for two reasons: impression and cost. The heavier the papers are, the more expensive the direct mail package will "feel." If you want to express an expensive, quality image, you want to use heavier papers. If you are mailing your package first class, exceeding one ounce raises the cost of the mailing significantly. If you are mailing standard class (bulk rate), you can mail up to 3 ounces for the same low price.

Papers come in different weights. To get an idea of different paper weights, compare newsprint with the pages of this book. Compare both of these with the cover of the book. Each is a different weight. Paper weight is indicated in pounds. The higher the number, the heavier the paper.

 Usually, you use between 50# (read 50 *pound*) and 70# paper for letters, 60–80# paper for brochures, and 90–105# matte-coated stock for order cards. Envelopes usually use 24# white wove. If you want to check the weight of your package, go to www.horah.com and use the weight calculator.

What about paper grade?

The brightness, smoothness, and whiteness are used to determine the *grade.* The brighter, smoother, and whiter a piece of white paper is, the better its quality. The best quality paper is called *premium grade.* From there, grades go down from #1 to #5, the least expensive.

To feel the difference in grades, place a sheet of paper from a weekly magazine and monthly magazine next to each other. You can easily see and feel the difference in the grades.

What about ink?

When you print, you put transparent ink on the paper; what you actually see is not ink, but the light reflecting *through* the ink onto the paper and back at you. The smoother the surface of the paper and the brighter the paper is, the better the final printed image will look (see the sections earlier in this chapter for more on paper).

Four-color process

If you are going to print full color photos or illustrations, you'll probably be printing with *process inks* (cyan, magenta, yellow, and black). Although four-color process is used to reproduce lifelike images of full-color photographs, it can reproduce only about 32,000 colors found in nature. As a result, many other colors can't be matched exactly with four-color process. That's when other inks, which are commonly identified with a number from the Pantone Matching System (PMS), come in handy (see the section "Spot colors" for details).

If you are using four color process and need to have a specific PMS color for a corporate color match, print with five colors. Most printers can accommodate this at very little additional expense.

Spot colors

If you're only using color to highlight type, such as headlines or paragraph heads, you might be using spot colors, sometimes called *PMS colors*. There are several thousand to choose from, and if your designer has not chosen any, your printer can help.

A good example illustrating the difference between the PMS system and four-color process is IBM blue. This color has a specific PMS number (PMS 287) that cannot be matched in process. Using four-color process, you can mix cyan and black and come close, but the color isn't quite the same.

Certain colors can lead to problems. For example, some blue colors, similar to IBM blue, don't dry well. If you are using a lot of it, you could have trouble with ink rubbing off onto other sheets (called *offsetting*). Pick colors that work together well and ask the printer if he thinks there will be any problems.

How the Presses Work

Eventually, you'll be ready to send your direct mail piece to be printed. Following are descriptions of how the presses that you'll usually use work.

- ✔ **Offset lithography:** The most common commercial presses today use a process called *offset lithography*. The image is photochemically etched onto a printing plate. Ink adheres to the plate where the images are, and the ink is transferred to a *blanket* (a rubber material like that found on a squeegee). The blanket transfers the ink to the paper. The paper never touches the plate, which is why it's called offset.

- ✔ **Flexography:** Many of the envelopes you get in the mail are printed through a process called flexography. This letterpress process uses plastic or rubber instead of metal printing plates — sort of like using a rubber stamp. Usually, a roll of paper, which we call a web, is put on the machine. The roll is first printed, and then the envelopes are cut out of the paper and folded all in one process. Finished envelopes come off the end of the machine.

- ✔ **Digital presses:** These presses all work directly from a digital file (see the section "Mastering the Prepress Process: Desktop Publishing," earlier in this chapter) and can produce four colors or more on both sides of the paper in one pass. Digital presses don't require plates, and they use different types of toners instead of ink.

    Digital presses are either *copiers,* where the information is fed into the press digitally and each sheet that is printed is the same for an entire job, or *variable digital presses.* The latter presses allow every document to be different, which means that you can personalize it. You can make every piece different based on the variable data in your database or list.

If you're using a variable digital press, you can also make your images different on each piece. A car dealer can have pictures of cars on the mailer he receives, and a barber can have pictures of barbershops on the piece he receives. This unique targeting helps to increase response rates because it draws the target prospect closer to the message. This type of press also allows for economical printing of very small lots.

Part III
Ready, Send, Results!

The 5th Wave   By Rich Tennant

SWIM WITH THE GIANT SQUID

SWIM WITH THE MORAY EELS

SWIM WITH THE JELLYFISH

SWIM WITH OCTOP

"Our 'Swim With' campaign isn't getting the response we'd hoped for. Maybe we should have just sent free keychains."

In this part . . .

After your mail piece is created, you're ready to get results. But first you have to master the mailing system. In this part, you not only find out how to do this, but you discover how to tally up your results as well.

Chapter 9

Delivering Your Direct Mail Piece

● ●

In This Chapter

▶ Taking advantage of money-saving postage strategies

▶ Making your mailing addresses consistent

▶ Getting rid of duplicate mailings

● ●

*A*fter you have your direct mail piece prepared, you may think your job is done. Not so fast. You still haven't placed your personalized creations into the homes of your target audience members . . . and that's what direct mail is all about!

An important player in your direct-mail success is the U.S. Postal Service. And if you play by its rules, not only will you save money, but you'll ensure that your direct mail is arriving where you want it to when you want it to: in the mailboxes of your potential buyers.

Saving Postage Money

Mailing your pieces is not just a matter of dropping them into a mailbox and waving bye-bye. If you're interested in saving money (and you probably are since you want to *make* money), then you can do several things that can decrease your postage costs.

Know your class

Just like flying on an airplane, you have the option of sending your mail first class. When you place your stamp on a letter and drop it in the nearest mailbox, you're mailing *first class.* With first class service, your letter should arrive anywhere in the country in one to three days. And if the person you're mailing to has moved within the past 12 to 18 months and left a forwarding address, your mail will find his or her new home at no extra charge. What a deal!

Standard class (soon to be called MarketMail and once known as third class) allows you to mail a minimum of 200 pieces of advertising mail at one time. Although you get lower bulk rates, your mail usually takes seven to ten days to arrive at its destination.

 If you use standard class, make sure that your addresses are as up to date as possible — your mail won't be forwarded if the recipients have moved.

Make the Postal Service's job easier

This moneysaving tip is kind of like the theory, *"You scratch my back, and I'll scratch yours."* The more work you do for the Postal Service, the greater discount you get. For example, if you are mailing first class and have a minimum of 500 pieces, you (or your lettershop) can sort your mail by zip code and get a discount. If you have 150 pieces going to the same first three digits of a zip code and you sort it properly, you get the 3-digit discount. If you have 150 pieces going to the same 5-digit zip code, you get the 5-digit discount, which is even more.

If your mail is automation-compatible, then you get a bigger discount. The cost to the Postal Service of processing an automatable letter is 4 cents, while processing a letter or card that you write by hand is 44 cents. Naturally, the Postal Service wants as much mail as possible to be automated. Your piece of mail needs to meet three criteria to be automation-compatible:

✔ Your addresses need to be CASS-certified addresses (see the section "Standardizing Your Mailing Addresses," later in this chapter).

✔ Your addresses need to have been updated.

✔ Your mailing pieces need to either be in the form of a letter or flat and meet the criteria outlined in Table 9-1.

Table 9-1	Physical Characteristics of Automated Mail Pieces		
Type	*Height*	*Length*	*Thickness*
First Class post card	3.5" min. / 4.25" max.	5" min. / 6" max.	.007 min. / .016 max.
Letters (all classes)	3.5" min. / 6.125" max.	5" min. / 11.5" max.	.009" min. / .25" max.
Flat-size mail	4" min. / 12" max.	4" min. / 15.75" max.	009" min. / 1.25" max.

Just like postage rates, the specifications in Table 9-1 can change from time to time. If you think the specifications may have changed, ask the Postal Service or check on the Web site www.horah.com for the latest specifications and rates.

Send deliverable mail

With almost 20 percent of the U.S. population moving every year, the chances are good that some of your addresses will be undeliverable. To get the best discounts on postage, you need to make sure that your mail is deliverable as addressed. If you want your first class rates discounted, you must use one of the following methods to double-check your addresses:

✔ **National Change of Address (NCOA) service:** This service ensures that your addresses are current and updates them to the most current addresses available for the recipients. Once again, your addresses must be standardized in order to find matches on the NCOA file (see the section "Standardizing Your Mailing Lists," later in this chapter). Fortunately, the NCOA process includes address standardization. The file keeps track of address changes for 36 months and chains multiple moves.

NCOA is the name of the file the postal service maintains of reported address changes that occurred in the past 36 months. The file is updated every 10 days. All direct mail computer service bureaus can offer the service of matching your names against this file to make sure you have the most current addresses on your mailing. The cost is negotiated by the vendor you select and will get less expensive as you increase the number of records you process. The cost can be anywhere from $5 per 1,000 to less than $1 per 1,000.

If you're going to perform a merge/purge, do it only after NCOA does its magic so that you're matching the latest addresses for everyone.

✔ **A service bureau:** Not only do service bureaus double-check your addresses, but certain ones, known as *presort bureaus,* can presort your mail and send it with many other company's mailings (called *commingling*) so that you get a bigger discount — just not as big as if you did all the work yourself.

✔ **A program called** *Fastforward: Fastforward* works off of a CD-ROM that contains all reported address changes for the past 12 months.

You don't have to double-check addresses to get a bulk rate discount, but, as noted earlier, your mail won't be forwarded. Remember: Checking is a lot cheaper than postage and printing.

Standardizing Your Mailing Addresses

If you want your mail to get to the correct place as quickly and cheaply as possible, you need to *standardize* your mailing addresses. Standardizing simply means that all your addresses are consistent. For example, if you live at 345 North Elm Street and you're following the postal service's rules of standardization, then your address should appear as 345 N Elm St (no periods).

Here are the standardization rules to remember when you're creating your addresses:

✔ Always use one or two letters for the directional — for example, use the letter *N* for North, *S* for South, and so on. Don't use a period.

✔ Use the fixed abbreviations for street, road, avenue, and so on. Table 9-2 lists the most common abbreviations, but there are hundreds of them. You can get a complete list from the Postal Service.

✔ Don't use any punctuation.

Table 9-2	Common Fixed Abbreviations
Type	*Abbreviation*
Street	St
Road	Rd
Boulevard	Blvd
Court	Ct
Lane	Ln

If standardization sounds like a task you'd rather not do, you're in luck. Not only do most mail houses and list processing service bureaus provide this service, but you can find services on the Internet as well. You can even find computer software, called CASS-certified, that does the job for you.

In order to get discounts for mailing large volumes of mail (200 pieces of bulk rate mail or 500 pieces of first class mail), your addresses must be CASS-certified.

Merging Your Mailing Lists

No one likes to receive multiple copies of the same piece of mail, even if the letters are personalized. But if you're using more than one mailing list, you probably will have the same people listed several times. Not only does mailing duplicates irritate the recipient, but it also wastes your money. Performing a merge-and-purge process, though, can help make your list duplicate-free.

You must standardize your addresses before performing a merge-and-purge because the addresses may not match otherwise. (See the preceding section for more on standardization.) If your addresses aren't standardized, the computer will not eliminate duplicates when it combines the mailing lists.

Keep in mind that although the computer is doing the work, you're the person who defines the matching process. Here are some questions to ask yourself when you determine your criteria:

- ✔ Are shortened versions of formal names — for example, Bob and Robert — located at the same address a match? Probably.

- ✔ Are similar sounding names, such as Richard Goldsmith and Richard Goldman, located at the same address a match? Probably, but you have to assume not.

- ✔ Are identical names at slightly different addresses — for example, 123 Main St versus 123 E Main St — a match? Probably.

- ✔ Do you want to send duplicates to *multibuyers* (people whose names appear on more than one list)?

Your goal is to wind up with a mailing list that does not contain identical names. If you are sending multiple letters to the same person, it's because you *decided* to do it, not because you made a mistake.

Why send duplicate mail pieces on purpose? Multibuyers!

A general rule is that if you send multibuyers the same piece of mail about two weeks after the initial mailing, you will get 50 percent of the response rate that you got the first time.

If you have left over mailing pieces (you should), and you've already paid for the names, your only additional cost on the second mailing is the postage. That makes this second mailing very profitable.

Sometimes you can make arrangements through your list broker with the list owners to only pay for the names you use. As a result, any duplicate names you eliminate are "return-able" because you're not using them.

Taking Advantage of Mailing Shops

If the thought of organizing and mailing hundreds, thousands, or even millions of pieces overwhelms you, don't despair. You can find help in the form of commercial lettershops. These shops, for a fee, help you with numerous services:

- ✓ **Addressing the mail:** Lettershops take your files and address your mail by either labeling, ink jetting, or laser-ing it. Show your lettershop manager what you're planning and rely on his advice about the best way to address your mail.

- ✓ **Bursting continuous forms, if used:** When your mailing is greater than 50,000 pieces, the piece with the address on it is often printed as a continuous form. That means the paper goes into the press as a roll and comes out as a roll or fan folded. This technique enables high-speed personalization equipment to be used for the addressing and other personalization. Bursting simply seperates one form from another.

- ✓ **Folding continuous forms, if necessary.**

- ✓ **Affixing stickers, cards, stamps, and tabs:** Using a machine called a Labelaire, lettershops can apply stickers and labels for you. They can also seal self-mailers and double postcards with tabs.

- ✓ **Inserting components into envelopes:** Machines in the lettershop usually can insert up to six different items into an envelope. The machines also seal the envelopes and sometimes even meter or stamp them as well.

- ✓ **Sorting and traying the mail for the Postal Service:** The lettershop bundles the mail according to Postal Service requirements, placing it in in trays if you're sending letter size mail or in sacks if your mail is flat.

   ✔ **Delivering the mail to the post office:** Your lettershop
      should get a receipt from the Postal Service, proving that
      your mail was accepted for mailing. Make sure that you
      keep that receipt, just in case you have any problems
      down the road.

 If you're mailing thousands of pieces, use a commercial lettershop to save time. Remember, your time is worth something,
and you may be better off spending it doing other tasks.

Chapter 10

Measuring Your Results

- -

In This Chapter

▶ Determining whether your direct mail campaign was a success or failure

▶ Discovering which offers work best for you

- -

*O*kay, your mailing is done. You're probably asking yourself, "Did it work? What kind of response should I expect?" Well, we're going to give you the answer you don't want to hear: There's no easy answer to this question! The answer depends on what you're selling, how you made your offer, and how well you targeted your list.

If you're confused about how to measure results, take heart. In this chapter, we give you several tips to help you answer this oft-asked question.

Knowing What Kind of Response to Expect

Many people are ecstatic when they get a 3 percent response. Others are disappointed. For responses to a prospect list, 3 percent is very good. If your offer is to your customers, you probably expected to do much better.

In evaluating response, you can't even go by the number of orders that you get. If you get tons of orders, you're probably doing okay — but maybe you're not. In the following sections, we give you a few techniques to help you determine whether you're getting the response you need and deserve.

Think about lifetime value

If you're like most people in direct mail, you have a catalog full of products you want to sell. Often, you don't make a profit on the initial sale to a customer. You're giving up your profit in the hopes that your first-time customer, over a period of time, will continue to buy more products — products from which you do earn a profit. In fact, you should think of your initial investment like a magazine subscription. The publisher loses money on new subscriber acquisition, but probably 60 to 80 percent of the subscribers renew. *That's* where the profit is.

What you're really interested in is the *lifetime value* of the customer — your total earnings from a customer. You need to estimate what this number will be *before* you embark on direct marketing as a business strategy. That number is what enables you to measure your *return on investment.*

A good predictor of lifetime value is a measurement called RFM — recency, frequency, and monetary value. When was the last time a customer made a purchase, how often does he or she purchase, and how much did he or she spend?

- ✔ **Recency:** If someone has recently purchased from you, then it's more likely that she will purchase again — assuming that she had a good experience, of course.
- ✔ **Frequency:** The more often that someone purchases, the more likely he will purchase from you again.
- ✔ **Monetary value:** The more a customer spends, the more valuable she is.

You use these measurements to decide which of your customers to mail to, how often, and what products to offer to them.

You must study your customers' buying behavior to know how to best apply these measurements for your future marketing efforts. You don't want to waste marketing dollars on people who become less and less likely to buy again. (See Chapter 5 for more on identifying your audience.)

The 80/20 rule

For many businesses, the 80/20 rule holds up: 80 percent of your sales come from only 20 percent of your customers. Analyze your *sales* results to see to what extent this maxim is true for you. Then, through testing, gradually *increase* the frequency of mailings to the portion of your market that produces the bulk of the sales and gradually *decrease* mailings to the rest. Done properly, this technique rebalances your budget so that you're investing in the more profitable segment of your database.

Next, analyze your *profit* results to determine which of your customers contribute 80 percent of your profits. Invest more of your promotional dollars in this most profitable segment and less in the less profitable customers.

Keep a database

If you maintain a good database, you can discover a lot about your customers and their buying habits, or lack thereof. (See the sidebar "The 80/20 rule.")

Keep careful track of everyone who responds to one of your mailings, no matter who that person is. Keep track of *everything* about that person, not just the name and address. What campaign and offer did he respond to? How often has he purchased? How much has he spent? When was the last purchase? Does he return a lot of the things he buys?

Your database can tell you a lot about your best customers, such as what they respond to and how profitable they are. And that will help you find customers just like them.

Testing the Waters: Measuring Your Responses

One of the great benefits of direct mail is that it's measurable. That means that you can find out what's working and what isn't. That also means that you can fix what's broken.

Imagine you're a retailer. If you send an invitation to prospects to visit your store, try including two different coupons for half of each mail. One can be for a free product, while the other can be for a 10 percent discount. Then count your returned coupons — which one brought more people to your store? You now know which promotion to use the next time you mail.

If you're sending direct mail, you need to test everything — offers, creativity, and lists. Be careful, however, about how you structure your tests. You can only test one thing at a time, or you won't know what part of your direct mail contributed to the results.

In most cases, for a statistically valid test, you need to get 100 responses. Determine what your normal response rate is and then use that number to figure out how many pieces to mail. For example, if you normally get a 5 percent response from a mailing that invites people to your store for an event, you would need to mail at least 2,000 pieces ($100 \times .05 = 5$ percent). If your response rate is 2 percent, you would need to mail to 5,000 people ($100 \times .02 = 2$ percent).

Keep in mind that your lists need to be accurate when you're doing this test. See Chapter 9 to find out how to make your addresses as up to date as possible.

Part IV
The Part of Tens

The 5th Wave | By Rich Tennant

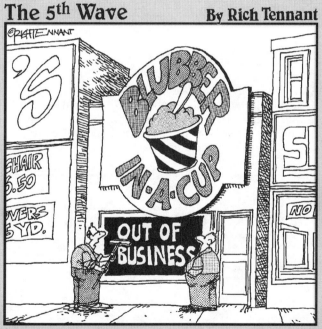

"It's hard to figure. The concept was a big hit in Nome."

In this part . . .

*A*re you ready for a little fun? Then sit down with The Part of Tens. We tell you ten people who definitely shouldn't be missing out on direct mail, as well as ten reasons why you don't have to be worried about the Internet thwarting your direct mail campaign.

Chapter 11

Ten People Who Should Be Using Direct Mail

. . . .

Direct mail isn't for everyone. But there are a lot of people in the world who should be taking advantage of this powerful tool but aren't. In this chapter, we give you ten or so people who could benefit from this tool. Are you one of them?

Entrepreneurs

If you're starting or running a business in any industry, direct mail is for you. You can't afford to miss out on the new customers that such a program can draw to your business.

Small Business Owners

Whether you're running a small business or one that's based in your home, direct mail can help bring you a steady supply of sales leads and customers who buy again and again. If you can identify your prospects on a mailing list, you can mail them offers that motivate them to inquire, look — and buy.

Retailers

If you're looking for new customers or want to strengthen relationships with your existing customers, you can benefit from the help of direct mail. You can create a powerful difference between you and your competitors by using mail to "personalize" your store, for example. Start by capturing the names and addresses of your customers at every transaction: Record the date, what they bought, and how much they spent. Then send simple "Thank you" notes with a savings coupon or discount offer for their next visit. They'll be back soon.

Professionals

Are you new to your field, offering new services, or building relationships with existing clients? Then try direct mail. Ask yourself what other professionals can refer clients to you (accountants and attorneys are natural networking buddies), and then mail to these people, inviting them to refer people to you. Another idea is to find mailing lists of prospects within a half-hour's drive; entice the people on this list with a free consultation or discount.

Sales Managers

If you're a sales manager, direct mail can help you find leads. Sending mail with the classic "free information" offer is far less expensive than sending out salespeople like unguided missiles. When prospects ask for information, they're essentially saying, "I'm about ready to buy."

Ad Managers

Direct mail can help ad managers in all types of companies — manufacturing, services, wholesaling, and distributing — extend their marketing efforts to key members of their customer base. Used in synch with print advertising, direct mail can leverage your ad budget. The simplest way is to mail copies of your latest ad to your best prospects and customers with text that says something like "I wanted to be sure you didn't miss our special offer (or whatever) on Wingless Widgets in Widget World Magazine. If you order within 15 days, take an extra 5% off!" In short, use the mail to hype the offer in your ad. You'll stand out from the other guys.

Marketing Managers

If you're a marketing manager in a highly competitive industry, such as banking, printing, transportation, pharmaceuti-
cals, publishing, recruiting, collectibles, and financial
services, direct mail can be your salvation. You'll be able to
regularly inform and remind your best prospects and customers about your services or products. Direct mail can help
you create a "value added" point of difference — personal
service. In price-competitive industries, someone is always
ready to undercut you. Go the other way. Use mail to offer
more value to your customers in terms of added personal or
technical service. This strategy is a proven way to justify
maintaining your prices. Remember, people want to know how
much you care before they care how much you charge.

Fundraisers

No matter what type of fundraiser you are — religious, educational, or nonprofit — you can gain income through direct
mail. For you, there are two types of mail: bottom and top. At
the bottom, you should be doing "donor acquisition" mailings,
finding new givers. You've got to keep growing your donor
base. At the top, use direct mail to thank and cultivate your
regular donors — especially big givers. Show you appreciate
their support and keep them informed and involved. The gifts
will keep coming.

CEOs and CFOs

If you're a CEO or CFO and need to make key strategic decisions about the growth and direction of your company, then
direct mail can give you a helping hand. Direct mail can be an
effective strategic tool to keep employees, prospects, customers, and suppliers informed and supportive whenever you
make changes. Direct mail helps keep your news personal and
shows you care about the people you work and do business
with. Done in a timely manner, direct mail prevents misunder-
standings, squelches rumors, and helps build loyalty and
cooperation, even when the news isn't all good.

Chapter 12

Ten Reasons Why the Internet Won't Kill Direct Mail

● ●

*M*uch is being written nowadays about the death of direct mail. What people are saying is that the Internet is making direct mail obsolete. Yeah, the Internet is making direct mail obsolete just like it's making television, radio, and telephones obsolete.

This chapter gives you a few less than ten reasons why it just ain't so.

Not Every Business Is Online

Granted, with all the media hype about the Internet, it's easy to believe otherwise. But in reality, naw.

Think about it: How many mailings do you get that invite you to visit a Web site? Many, yes. But not all. Fact is, a lot of mail you get doesn't have a Web address on it. And a lot of physical stores don't have virtual stores on the Web.

Not everyone looks to the Internet for all of his or her needs and answers.

Direct Mail Is Personal

This one's a no-brainer. You can curl up with a good letter, just like a good book, *whenever* and *wherever* you want. You don't have to read it from a screen while always sitting in one derned place — in front of an impersonal computer.

People want that personal touch. They aren't going to give it up.

The Statistics Show Growth

The Direct Marketing Association predicts that direct mail volume will increase at a rate of 6.4 percent annually for many years to come. That's a healthy growth rate — about double the typical rate of the U.S. economy as a whole.

They Actually Work Together

When television was invented, people predicted the demise of the movie industry. We all know that hasn't happened. In fact, movies are one of television's biggest advertisers. The TV and movie industries are working together. And that's what's already happening with the Internet and direct mail.

With careful planning, you can effectively integrate the Internet and direct mail:

- You can use direct mail to do things like promote Web sites, reach people who don't use the Internet, and fulfill Web site requests for more information.

- You can use the Internet to build a list of prospects that want more information about your product (and then include them in your next mailing). And you can use the Internet as a solid, wide-ranging resource. For example, you can find innovative, cost-effective services on the Internet that help you produce your mail, clean and process your lists, rent compiled lists, and get all kinds of information about direct mail.

Index

D

database, 91
database services, 36–37
delayed payments, 32
deliverable mail, 83–84
design
  color, 67–68
  fonts, 68
  word-processing program, 68–69
desktop publishing, 71
digital presses, 77
dimensional package, 53
direct mail, 1, 8–9
  accomplishments, 25
  actions, 25
  booklets, 47
  business-to-business sellers, 53
  catalogs, 47
  costs, 19
  design, 57
  designing graphics, 23
  double postcards, 44–45
  ease of response, 22–23
  effectiveness of, 9–10
  extent of, 10
  finalizing copy and graphic
    design, 24
  fund-raisers, 34
  identifying target audience, 22
  items that fail in, 10–11
  keeping and filing, 19
  mailing, 81–84
  marketing or sales strategy, 22
  no-win scenario, 16
  offers, 23, 29–30
  paper, 23
  as personal medium, 9
  personal messages, 10
  postal service specifications and
    rates, 24
  postcards, 43–44
  production methods, 23
  product or service to offer, 22
  responses, 89–91

rough-draft copy, 23
self-mailers, 45–46
steps for creating, 21–25
testing, 24
tracking orders, 24
type of response, 22–23
vendors, 23
writing, 56
direct mail package, 47
  brochure, 50
  buck slips, 52–53
  envelope, 48–49
  flyers, 52
  letter, 49–50
  lift letters, 53
  magalogs, 53
  order form with reply device,
    51–52
  stickers, 52–53
direct marketing, 8–9
  versus advertising, 11–13
  AIDA (Attention, Interest, Desire,
    and Action), 12
  channel of distribution, 12
Direct Marketing Association, 56
Direct Marketing Magazine, 37
distribution channels, 12
DMA (Direct Marketing
  Association), 10
DM News, 37
double postcards, 44–45
dummy, 47

E

effectiveness of direct mail, 9–10
envelopes
  direct mail package, 48–49
  reply device, 51
everyday language, 61
exclusivity, 33
extended payments, 32

(continued)

U

unbelievable offers, 33
uncoated paper, 74–75
uncoated text paper, 75

V

variable digital presses, 77–78
vendors, 23
visualizing audience, 57

W

word-processing program, 68–69
wove paper, 74
writing
 asking for order, 61
 being specific, 65
 choosing words carefully, 64–65
 everyday language, 61
 features benefiting reader, 61
 focusing on benefits, not features,
  58–60
 friendliness, 58
 getting reader involved, 60
 grammar, 63–64
 leasing *versus* buying, 62
 motivating people to action,
  60–62
 personal copy, 58
 postscript, 62
 power words, 65
 presenting benefit before
  information, 60
 sentence and paragraph length,
  62–63
 structure of, 62–64
 visualizing audience, 57
wrong mailing lists, 39

Y

Yes/No option stickers, 52–53

Notes

Notes

Notes

. . . .

Notes

Notes

Notes